MODELS OF TEACHING

MODEL OF TEACHING

S.P. Bhattacharya
with the assistance of
Sarbari Baksi | Purnima Basu

2025
Regency Publications
A Division of
Astral International Pvt. Ltd.
New Delhi – 110 002

First Published, 1994
Reprinted, 2025

ISBN: 978-81-86030-03-5

Disclaimer:

Every possible effort has been made to ensure that the information contained in this book is accurate at the time of going to press, and the publisher and author cannot accept responsibility for any errors or omissions, however caused. No responsibility for loss or damage occasioned to any person acting, or refraining from action, as a result of the material in this publication can be accepted by the editor, the publisher or the author. The Publisher is not associated with any product or vendor mentioned in the book. The contents of this work are intended to further general scientific research, understanding and discussion only. Readers should consult with a specialist where appropriate.

Every effort has been made to trace the owners of copyright material used in this book, if any. The author and the publisher will be grateful for any omission brought to their notice for acknowledgment in the future editions of the book.

Published by : **Regency Publications**
A Division of
Astral International Pvt. Ltd.
– ISO 9001:2015 Certified Company –
4736/23, Ansari Road, Darya Ganj
New Delhi-110 002
Ph. 011A43549197, 23278134
E-mail: info@astralint.com
Website: www.astralint.com

At the Lotus Feet of my teacher Professor M.B. Buch, D.Litt. Formerly Head, Centre of Advunced Study in Education, M.S. University of Baroda, India.

- Siba -

THEN said a teacher, Speak to us of Teaching.
And he said:
No man can reveal to you aught but that which already lies half asleep in the dawning of your knowledge.
The teacher who walks in the shadow of the temple, among his followers, gives not of his wisdom but rather of his faith and his lovingness.
If he is indeed wise he does not bid you enter the house of his wisdom, but rather leads you to the threshold of your own mind.
The astronomer may speak to you of his understanding of space, but he cannot give you his understanding.
The musician may sing to you of the rhythm which is in all space, but he cannot give you the ear which arrests the rhythm, nor the voice that echoes it.
And he who is versed in the science of numbers can tell of the regions of weight and measure, but he cannot conduct you thither.
For the vision of one man lends not its wings to another man.
And even as each one of you stands alone in God's knowledge, so must each one of you be alone in his knowledge of God and in his understanding of the earth.

Kahlil Gibran,
The Prophet

FOREWORD

The contemporary research in social sciences is characterised by a distinct emphasis on developing theories in their respective fields. In the special field of educational research, efforts to develop a theory of teaching has been noticed since Barr's (1929) pioneering work on teacher effectiveness. The publication of Gage's *Handbook* in 1963 was a landmark development on theory building in teaching. Teaching had been taken up as one major area of research in the *Centre of Advance Study in Education* (CASE) in 1971. A band of researchers started working on various aspects of it. Their work was directed towards developing a serviceable, scientific theory of teaching, especially in Indian conditions. S.P. Bhattacharya came to CASE in 1971 to study on theory of teaching and in 1973 the Centre published his monograph of 'Research on Theory of Teaching' and he did his Ph.D. under my supervision on Micro-teaching in 1975. He has been studying the theory of teaching for last twenty years and he knows thoroughly the developments in theory building in India and abroad.

He has written this book for the students of Education at graduate and post-graduate levels. In his book he has comprehensively dealt with concepts, principles of teaching and models of teaching; he has described different, widely used models of teaching and the families of the models. Also, in short, he depicts the endeavors in India in building and using models of teaching. I feel very happy to see that he is introducing my friend, Shib K. Mitra's 'Model of Teaching,' which is a unique Indian contribution in this field.

Educationists like Mitra gave us all support, when research in teaching was attempted to be put on a systematic basis by the Centre of Advanced Study in Education, M.S. University of Baroda during seventies. During that decade systematic research in teacher behaviour and theory of teaching was undertaken.

Four *Surveys of Research in Education* included trend reports related to research in teaching. The first trend report received 21 studies on teaching. Second trend report classified the studies into three groups, viz. teacher behaviour studies, tool construction studies and other studies. The teacher behaviour studies were further classified as presage-process studies, process-product studies and presage-process-product studies. Whatever the nature of classification, process-product studies are important as manipulating processes, product can be changed. The society is concerned with the product of teaching. About two decades have passed since the first monograph on Bhattacharya's *Review of Research on Theory of Teaching* (1973) was published. Still the researchers have not been able to give a valid theory/theories of teaching. But the research had led us to a point where it may not be difficult to come to a conclusion regarding concepts and propositions about models of teaching. In the mean time practitioners have devised their own approach of teaching and the phenomenon goes on in the classrooms.

Twenty years have not gone in vain. Teaching has improved with the knowledge of theories of teaching. Let us hope that it is not long before a theory or theories of teaching is developed by researchers in the field. This is the significance of the beginning of systematic research in seventies.

Finally I bless Siba, my dear student for the last twenty years and ever, for writing this excellent book for the students and practitioners of teaching.

M.B. BUCH

46, Harinagar,
Gotri Road,
Baroda 390007
Dewali
13th November, 1993.

PREFACE

Models of Teaching have been incorporated in the revised syllabuses of the B.Ed., M.Ed. and M.A./M.Sc. courses in Educational Indian Universities. It is also included in the syllabus of M.Phil. courses newly started. Models of Teaching is a content element in Papers like "Educational Technology," "Instructional Sciences" or "The Psychology of Learning and Instruction" in syllabuses of the Education courses, both in Under-graduate and Post-graduate levels in Indian universities. The book is written for students of Education course in an Indian University in general. It deals comprehensively in simple language with definitions, nature and concepts like "teaching", "model" and "model of teaching". Then it describes the approaches in model building in teaching as well as different families of models of teaching. In a subsequent section it describes 19 basic, widely used models, including an Indian model. The book concludes with Indian research and practice in models of teaching. Up-to-date comprehensive bibliography is given at the end of each chapter for those who want to study/research in this area.

I hope the students of Education will find this book as a good text and the Teachers of Education will use it as a reference material.

I am thankful to my co-authors in assistance Purnima Basu and Sarbari Baksi, who happen to be my students; I am also indebted to my Ph.D. Scholar Swapna Ghosh, for her all-out help in the preparation of the manuscript.

Professor M.B. Buch, the eminent Educationist and my revered Teacher, has kindly written a Foreword to this book.

Finally I dedicate this book to my Teacher Dr. Buch, who has been ever benevolent to his hundreds of students like me all over this country.

S.P. Bhattacharya

Deptt. of Education,
University of Calcutta,
Alipore Campus, Calcutta-700027.
January 15, 1994.

CONTENTS

CHAPTER ONE

CONCEPTS

1.1 TEACHING

There has been a lot of confusion regarding the concept of teaching and how teaching should be defined. If we take teaching as a complex human act performed by complex human organism and directed towards more complex human organism (students) in the complex situation called the classroom, it is still not clear how to give a precise definition of teaching. It may be interesting to quote Barr (1961) who said, "Teaching means many different things; and "that teaching act varies from person to person and from situation to situation." This confusion on the definition and concept of teaching will be clear from the following representative samples of the definitions of teaching.

> "*Teach*: impart knowledge or skill; give instruction or lesson, instil, inspire with."
>
> (*Little Oxford Dictionary*)

> "*Teaching*: the art of assisting another to learn. It includes the providing of information (instruction) and of appropriate situations, conditions or activities designed to facilitate learning."
>
> (*English & English 1958*)

"...teaching is system of action involving an agent, a situation, an end in view, and two sets of factors in the situation—one set over which the agent has no control, for example, size of class room and physical characteristics of pupils and another set which the agent can modify with respect to the end-in-view (for example, assignments and ways of asking questions).

(*Smith B.O. 1963*)

"Teaching behaviour, by its very nature, exists in a context of social interaction. The acts of teaching lead to reciprocal contacts between the teacher and the pupils, and the interchange itself is called teaching."

(*Flanders N.A. 1970*)

"...arranging the conditions of learning that are external to the learner. These conditions need to be constructed in a stage-by-stage manner, taking due account of each stage of the just previously acquired capabilities of the learner, the requirements for retention of these capabilities and the specific stimulus situation needed for the next stage of learning."

(*Gagne, R.M. 1965*)

"Teaching is the arrangement of contingencies or reinforcement under which students learn. They learn even without 'teaching' in their natural environments but teaching involves arranging of special contingencies which expedite learning, hastening the appearance of behaviour which would otherwise be acquired slowly or making sure of the appearance of behaviour which might otherwise never occur."

(*Skinner, B.F. 1968*)

"By teaching, we mean...any interpersonal influence aimed at changing the ways in which other persons can or will behave. This restriction to interpersonal influence is intended to rule out physical (e.g. mechanical), physiological, or economic ways of influencing another's behaviour, such as pushing him, dragging him or depriving him of a job. Rather the influence has to impinge on the other person through his perceptual and cognitive processes, i.e. through his ways to infer meaning out of objects and events that his sense make him aware of."

(*Gage, N.L. 1963*)

These definitions may be broadly classified into three types as mentioned by Mitra (1970):

i) It is imparting knowledge of skill.
ii) It is doing anything and everything that may lead to learning.
iii) It is a social act of influence.

N.L. Gage (1964) mentioned that 'teaching' is a misleading generic term: it covers too much. 'Instruction' is, therefore, defined as 'a special kind of teaching that has specificity of purpose and an orderliness, that does not characterise all teaching.' Teaching, learning and instruction are clearly not interchangeable concepts. This relationship is reflected in Figure 1.1.

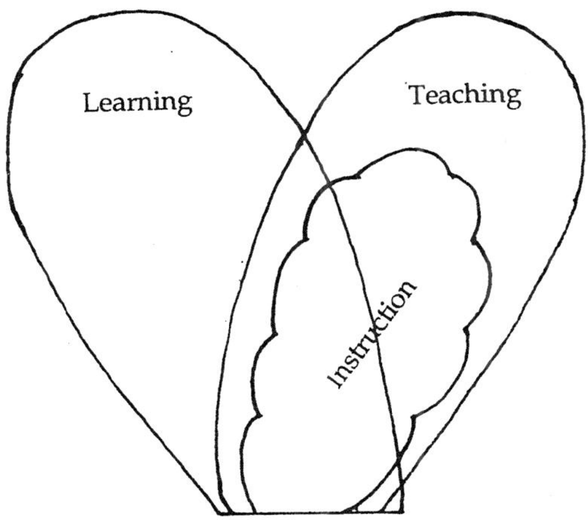

Fig. 1.1 Relationship between Teaching, Learning and Instruction

The considerations of viewing instruction as a special, but major case of teaching are:

i) the 'specifiability' of the behaviour to be learned as well as the conditions appropriate for that behaviour;
ii) the 'degree of control' exercised over the environment to the end that those behaviours will be brought under the control of appropriate situation.

Instruction is defined operationally as the 'process whereby the environment of an individual is deliberately manipulated to enable him to learn to emit or engage in specified behaviour under specified conditions or as responses to specified situations.'

Green's (1964) topology of teaching indicated four distinct stages as shown in Figure 1.2.

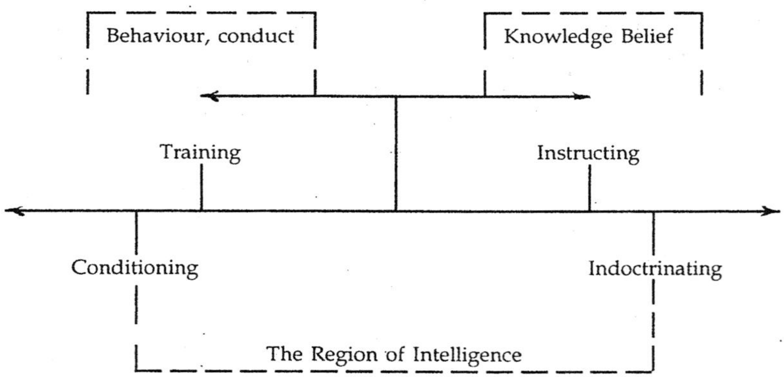

Fig. 1.2 The Teaching Continuum of Green

a) Training,
b) Conditioning,
c) Instructing, and
d) Indoctrinating.

The distinction between the four concepts is not clear and precise. Green opines that the structure of teaching should be interpreted in terms of components of teaching. Once we perceive the components, we shall be in a position to draw the topology of teaching and deduce a set of rules for teaching.

Training is a kind of teaching. In training the expression of the learner's intelligence is restricted. He is to obey certain orders. The trainer does not give reasons and the trainee also does not ask for it. Training is used to develop skills or conduct.

Conditioning is also a sort of training, which has a limited objective of developing a sort of blind habit. Instruction is an important type of teaching. It involves a kind of conversation, the object of which is to give reasons, weigh evidence, justify, explain and come to a conclusion.

Instruction is an important member of the family of activities called teaching.

Instruction seems, at heart, to involve a kind of conversation, the object of which is to give reasons, weigh evidence, justify, explain, conclude and so forth. It is true that whenever we are involved in giving instruction, it follows that we are engaged in teaching: but it is not true that whenever we are engaged in teaching we are giving instruction.

Instruction involves a kind of conversation, a giving of reasons, evidence, and so on, it is, therefore, unlike training, an activity allied to the acquisition of knowledge and belief than to the promotion of habits and modes of behavior. If the goal of teaching is the pursuit of truth, instruction is then central in the process of teaching.

Indoctrination means an extreme type of teaching. It is like conditioning of belief. But it is different from Training, Conditioning and Instructions, in that its curriculum produces plans for further action and hence is an obvious distinction to instruction which puts plans into action.

1.2 MODEL

The dictionary meaning of theory is "supposition to account for something; system of rules and principles, rules and reasoning etc. as distinguished from practice." (Collins English General Dictionary 1960)

Ryan, D.G. (1965) identified two types:

1) the axiomatic or hypothetico-deductive type and
2) the empirical, inductive type.

Maccia (1965) referred to:

1) formal theory—theory of pure logic and pure mathematics and
2) descriptive theory—theory of philosophy.

The Encyclopaedia Britanica (Vol. 22, 1964) gave under "Theory":

> It signifies a systematic account of some field of study, derived from a set of general propositions. These propositions may be taken as postulates, as in pure mathematics (theory of function etc.) or they may be principles more or less strongly confirmed by experience as in natural science (theory of heat, electromagnetic theory).

Gage (1963) wrote about theory in his Handbook as thus:

> "In this chapter, we use the term theory in a modest sense— to refer to any systematic ordering of ideas about the phenomena of a field of inquiry. We use the term in antithesis to ad-hoc, disorderly planning or interpretation of research..."

Model is an analogous term that helps scientists to arrange their findings and see important relations among them. Most scientists, however, prefer the term 'paradigm' to 'model' as it refers to a set of basic assumptions that outline the universe of scientific inquiry specifying both the concepts regarded as legitimate and the methods to be used in collecting and interpreting data.

1.3 MODEL OF TEACHING

A model of teaching is a plan or pattern that can be used to shape curricula, to design instructional materials and to guide instruction in the class room and other settings. The most important function of any model of teaching is to improve the instructional effectiveness in an interactive situation of curriculum transaction. Smith (1963) says:

"A theory of teaching will consist in (a) a statement of the variables comprising teaching behaviour, (b) a formulation of the possible relations among these variables, and (c) hypothesis about the relations between the variables comprising teaching behaviour and the variables descriptive of the psychological and social conditions within which teaching behaviour occurs."

Duke (1990) says:

"A teaching model is a comprehensive approach to teaching that typically derives from a theory of education and encompasses key assumptions about what students should learn and how they learn. Sometimes instructional models have been extensively researched; in other cases relatively little is known about their actual effectiveness. Models stress certain instructional functions and require teachers to be trained in particular ways. Some models are compatible with other models; some are apt to extol their virtues. It is reasonable to assume that no model is universally appropriate. Each possesses its own strengths and weaknesses."

In fine, it may be said that the theory of teaching should consist of general principles which have been derived from the experiences of teachers' observations of the classroom as well as from experimental evidence and reason.

References

English, H.B. and English, A.C. (1968): *Comprehensive Dictionary of Psychological and Psychoanalytical terms*, Longmans Green, New York.

Flanders, N.A. (1970): *Analyzing Teaching Behaviour*, Addison Wesley Publishing Company, Reading, Mass.

Gage, N.L.(Ed.) (1963): *Handbook of Research on Teaching*, Rand McWally and Co., Chicago.

Gagne, R.M. (1965): *Learning*, Holt, Rinehart and Winston, Inc., New York.

Green, T.F. (1964): "A Topology of the Teaching Concept," *Studies in Philosophy and Education*, 3, 284, Winter.

Mitra, S.K. (1970): "Psychology of Teaching: Rudiments of a Theory," Presidential Address, Psychology and Educational Science Section, 57th Indian Science Congress, IIT, Kharagpur, India.

Ryans, D.G. (1965): "A Model of Instruction based on Information System Concept," in James B. and Leeper, Robert R. (Eds.) *Theories of Instruction*, Association for Supervision and Curriculum Development, National Education Association, Washington D.C.

Skinner, B.F. (1968): *The Technology of Teaching*, Appleton-Century Crofts, New York.

Smith, B.O. (1963): "Toward A Theory of Teaching," in Bellack, A.A. (Ed.), *Theory and Research in Teaching*, Bureau of Publications, Teachers College, Columbia University, New York.

CHAPTER TWO

RATIONALE

2.1 NEED FOR A MODEL OF TEACHING

The utility of a theory of teaching in research on teaching may be summed up as follows. "It is a guide to the formation of research hypotheses that may be tested in practical context. It trains investigators to look for facts which may not be readily apparent. It cumulates research work, allowing old studies to gain support from new studies."

It also allows research to proceed systematically. Above all, it makes possible the conclusions to take short-hand form and thereby help communicability among the researchers themselves and also between the researchers and the practitioners in teaching.

One might ask the question why the teachers need a theory of instruction, since psychology already contains theories of learning and development. Bruner (1966) says in this connection, that the teachers do not need a descriptive theory, which learning theories really are, but they need a prescriptive theory.

"...theories of learning and development are descriptive rather than prescriptive. They tell us what happened after the fact, for example, that most of children of six do not yet possess the notion of reversibility. A theory of instruction, on the other hand, might attempt to set forth the best means of teaching the child towards the notion of reversibility. A theory of instruction, in short, is concerned with how what one wishes to teach can best be learned, with improving rather than describing learning."

About the role of theory as systemizer and binder of research of efforts, the report of the Committee on the Criteria of Teacher Effectiveness (1953) says:

> "... at present, research, too often, proceeds without explicit theoretical framework, in intellectual disarray, to the testing of myriads of arbitrary, unrationalized hypotheses. The studies too often interact little with each other, do not fall into place within any scheme and hence add little to the understanding of teaching process."

The committee, therefore, concerned itself with theories and paradigms with a view to draw notice to the necessity of more systematic and orderly approaches to the research on teaching.

As tools, theories allow the research worker to bring clarity into his concept, order in his procedure and system in his investigation.

Guba and Gatzels (1955) write:

> "a theoretical framework sharpens research objectives and suggests which variables may be eliminated being non-meaningful and hence wasteful, increases the likelihood of significant findings, simplifies the complex task of interpreting results, and makes research cumulative from one study to the next."

Kerlinger (1964) is also appreciative of the contemporary trend in building theories in Education. He says, that the development of theory should be the basic aim of research in Education. Theories, he contends, have wider applicability and usefulness than non-theoretical findings do.

> "Theories, because they are general, apply widely to many phenomena and to many people in many places. A specific relation, of course is less widely applicable."

In short the need for theory of instruction may be summarized as follows:

i) A theory of teaching helps to clarify the description of the teaching situation in ordinary language.

ii) It summarizes existing knowledge.
iii) It mediates applications of our knowledge of teaching to new situations.
iv) It leads to fruitful line of experimental inquiry.

2.2 THE NATURE OF A MODEL OF TEACHING

The term theory is used in teaching as "it is used in the natural science to represent a set of interrelated generalizations derived from data, which permit some degree of prediction or control over the phenomena to which they pertain." [Association for Supervision and Curriculum Development, NEA, Commission on Instructional Theory (1968).]

In this monograph the word 'teaching' refers mainly to the activity which takes place during schooling and within classroom setting. The term includes both material variables and human variables. It refers to the interaction between teacher, pupils and situational elements.

Bruner (1966) has prepared some valuable notes on a Theory of Instruction. He says:

> "A theory of instruction is 'prescriptive' in the sense that it sets for the rules concerning the most effective way of achieving knowledge or skill. By the same token it provides a yardstick for criticizing or evaluating any particular way of teaching or learning."

> "A theory of instruction is a 'normative' theory. It sets up criteria and states the condition for meeting them. The criteria must have a high degree of generality."

Bruner (1968) further elaborates the 'prescriptive' and 'normative' characteristics of theory of instruction in the following words:

> "Such a theory has the aim of achieving particular ends and producing them in ways that we speak of an optimal. It is not a description of what has happened, when learning has taken place—it is something which is normative, which gives you something to shoot at and which,

> in the end, must state some thing about what you do when you put instruction together in the form of courses."

Travers (1966) conceives of a theory of instruction as consisting of a set of propositions stating relationships, between, on the one hand, measures of the outcome of education and, on the other hand measures of both the conditions to which the learner is exposed and the variables representing characteristics of the learner.

He classifies the major independent variables of his model into four main classes:

— pupil variables;
— pupil task variables;
— teacher variables; and
— teacher task variables.

Following the same vein as of Bruner and Travers, Maccia (1965) writes:

> "To theorize about instruction, therefore, involves a choice as to whether the organized account shall be of instruction as it is or as it ought to be. Shall the theory be a scientific or a philosphic one? I selected the former alternative. The reason for the selection is that without a means of control, ideas as to how the phenomena we are dealing with are, related, we have no basis for implementing a philosophic theory of instruction, no matter how adequate that philosophic theory might be. A scientific theory of instruction, if adequate, provides such a basis."

Bruner (1968) has proposed that there are four aspects of such a theory.

First, a theory of instruction should concern itself with the factors that pre-dispose a child to learn effectively. These factors relate to his earliest childhood experience and these precede the child's entry into our scholastic care.

The second aspect of the theory of instruction is that it should concern itself with the optimal structuring of knowledge. By this he means that for any body of knowledge there is a minimal set of propositions, or statements, or images from which one can best generate the rest of what exists within that field. For example, from the conservation theorems plus a little more, a great deal of physics can be re-constructed.

A third aspect of a theory of instruction deals with the optimal sequence that is required for learning. In what order do we present things?... What exercises do you give the student to strengthen the views of his own thinking? What type of representation do you use? How much particular? How much generality?

Finally, a fourth aspect of a theory of instruction should concern itself with the nature and pacing of rewards and punishments and successes and failures.

To sum up then, a theory of instruction should be constructed around four problems: pre-dispositions, structures, sequences, and consequences. Travers holds that data of such a theory must be closely related to the phenomena of the classroom. The dependent variables of the system should be specified in terms of tasks and not in terms of behaviour. Then a useful taxonomy of objectives will involve a taxonomy of tasks. The task characteristics should further be directly observable.

2.3 APPROACHES IN BUILDING MODELS OF TEACHING

There are basically five approaches in building a theory of teaching. These five approaches can be grouped in two categories: Quantitative (that which looks at the relationship between observable teacher behavior and student achievement) and qualitative (that which is descriptive and seeks to understand the reasons why teaching is the way it is).

The three quantitative approaches are:

- — process-product approach;
- — the aptitude-treatment-interaction approach; and
- — the Carroll Model.

The process-product approach tries to find the relationship between teacher behaviour and the average amount of learning or achievement accomplished by a group. A typical process-product type would count the frequency with which a specific teacher behaviour or set of behaviours occurred in many classrooms over a fixed period of time. Then the frequency of teacher behaviour would be statistically correlated with average student achievement scores to determine the cause-effect relationships.

The aptitude-treatment-interaction approach on the other hand, is concerned with identifying particular instructional methods, that are well-suited to particular students. The guiding question of this type of a model is "which teaching method is best for which kinds of students."

The *Carroll Model* focuses on "time" as the most important factor in student achievement. This type of teaching investigates the ways for teachers to optimize the amount of time that students spend on learning tasks.

> The two qualitative approaches are cognitive information processing; and ethnography.

The cognitive information-processing approach deals with the basic psychological processes that organize and direct teacher behaviour. In studies of teacher planning for example, one can investigate how teachers' thoughts are translated into action in the classroom.

Ethnography, which has its roots in anthropology, looks at a whole social system (in this case, a classroom or a school) and portrays it in terms understood by its participants. Ethnographers frequently participate in the social system they are studying.

References

Bruner, J.S. (1966): *Toward A Theory of Instruction*, Harvard University Press, Cambridge, Mass.

Bruner, J.S. (1968): "Needed: A theory of Instruction," in Blackington III and Patterson, Robert S. (Eds.) *School, Society and the Professional Educator*, Holt, Rinehart and Winston, Inc., New York.

Guba, E. and Getzels, J.W. (1955): "Personality and Teacher Effectiveness: A Problem in Theoretical Research," *Journal of Educational Psychology*, 46, 330.

Kerlinger, F.N. (1964): *Foundations of Behavioural Research*, Holt, Rinehart and Winston, Inc., New York.

Travers, R.W. (1966): "Towards Taking the Fun out of Building a Theory of Instruction," Teachers College Record, 68, 49.

CHAPTER THREE

FAMILIES OF MODELS OF TEACHING

3.1 OVERVIEW ON MODELS OF TEACHING

Anderson (1969) classified the researchers on teaching theory into two broad categories:

i) Describers like Bellack (1966), Flanders (1965), Smith (1963), Jackson (1966) and the like;
ii) Improvers like Glaser (1965), Skinner (1968), Stolurow (1965) and the like.

Describers see improvers as tampering with humanistic values and improvers see the describers hopelessly bent upon improving the knowledge of obsolescent forms. In between describers and improvers are found to be a handful of researchers like Bruner (1966), Travers (1966), Gage (1969), and others who are more oriented towards prediction and control. They have taken their data from the describers' hypotheses and the characteristics of comprehensiveness, reliability and operationalism from improvers' experimentations. The author intends to call them empiricists who, he hopes, will influence the research of tomorrow on theories of teaching most.

Joyce and Weil (1992) developed more than 20 models which were grouped on the basis of their chief emphasis—why they approached educational goals and means. They have classified all the models into four families.

A. Information Processing Models

This family of models emphasizes onthe information processing capability of students and onthe systems that can improve their information processing capability. Information processing refers to the ways people handle stimuli from the environment, organise data, sense problems, generate concepts and solution to problems, and employ verbal and non-verbal symbols. Some of these models are concerned with the ability of the learners to solve problems, others with general intellectual ability of the learners. Some models of this family are:

— Inductive Thinking Model by Hilda Taba;
— Inquiry Training Model by Richard Suchman; and
— Concept Attainment Model by Jerome Bruner.

B. Behaviour Modification Models

This family has evolved from attempts to develop efficient system for sequencing learning tasks and shaping behaviour by manipulating reinforcement. Skinner (1958) has developed these models and operant conditioning is their central mechanism. It is represented by a large number of models, some of which are media-oriented (such as programmed strategies) and some of which are oriented to interactive teaching (such as the use of tokens to shape social behaviour). Some Models of this family are:

— Programmed Instruction Model by Crowder;
— Contingency Management Model by B.F. Skinner.

C. Social Interaction Models

This family share an orientation towards the relationships of the individual to society or to other persons. With respect to goals, models from this orientation give priority to the improvement of the individual's ability to relate to others, the improvement of democratic processes, and the improvement of the society. Some models of this family are:

— Classroom Meeting Model by Willium Glasser;
— Jurisprudential Model by James. P. Shaner and Donald Oliver; and
— Group Investigation Model by Herbert Thelen and John Dewey.

D. Personal Models

The models in this family share an orientation towards the individual and the development of selfhood. They emphasise the processes by which individuals construct and organise their unique reality. Some models of this family are:

— Nondirective Model by Carl Rogers;
— Synecties Model by Willium Gordon; and
— Conceptual Systems Model by David Hunt.

These families of models are by no means antithetical or mutually exclusive. The models classified in different families have common features both with respect to goals and to the kind of means they recommend. Most of our experiences, especially educational ones, involve some intellectual or information processing activity.

In the same way nearly all the models from the Information Processing Family are concerned with social relationships and the development of an integrated, functioning self.

Dunkin (1987) has classified the models of teaching in eight types, namely:

i) Human Interaction Models;
ii) Aptitude—Treatment Interaction Models;
iii) Behavioral Models;
iv) The Carrol Models;
v) Information Processing Models;
vi) Linguistic Models;
vii) Mastery Learning Models;
viii) Models of Heuristic Teaching.

In the *Introduction* he has outlined these models as follows:

> Models of teaching vary according to whether they are primarily concerned with the way teaching is or with the way teaching ought to be. The former models, the *descriptive* ones, are models in the sense of being attempts to portray the nature of teaching so that it might be better understood. They are representations of reality often highlighting some parts rather than others and offering particular perspectives that are abstracted from the whole. No one of them gives the complete picture but together

> they provide a comprehensive view. The other types of models, the *prescriptive* ones, are models in a different sense. They are there to be modeled, for teachers to model their teaching on, as prescriptions to be implemented. Sometimes they have been devised with a particular type of educational objective in mind, such as discovery learning. Sometimes they are applications to teaching of principles arising from a particular theory of learning, such as reinforcement theory.

The first models discussed are the *Human Interaction Models* in general.

The second approach is the *Aptitude-Treatment Interaction (ATI) Model* which is designed to take into account individual differences among learners in their readiness to benefit from instruction. This type of model involves matching instructional programmes with learner aptitudes in recognition of the fact that some teaching methods are more suitable for some students than for others.

The third model of teaching is the *Behavioural Model* which is based on reinforcement theory.

In the fourth model, time is of the essence. The *Carroll Model* of school learning is based on the idea that learning at a desired level will occur provided the learner spends the required amount of time at the learning task. The elaboration of the concept of time in learning is especially valuable and involves concepts of "opportunity"—the time allowed, "perseverance"—the time the learner is willing to spend, and "aptitude"—the amount of time needed under ideal conditions.

Information Processing Models of teaching include those which focus on teacher thinking, student thinking, and interaction between the two. They assume that the mental processes of teachers and students influence events in the classroom. Furthermore, they offer scope for explaining variations in learning which do not seem to conform to behavioural models.

Teacher focused models are models of teachers' interactive decision making, teachers' judgments, the "advance organizer" model of teaching, and inquiry teaching. Student focused models are a model of tutoring, computer-assisted instruction, a concept attainment model of instruction.

Linguistic Models of teaching are based upon the realization that verbal communication is the most noticeable feature of classroom interaction.

Mastery Learning Models are predominantly prescriptive. There are two basic characteristics of mastery approaches. One is a philosophical assertion that any teacher can help all students to learn "excellently, quickly, and self-confidently." The other is a set of ideas and procedures of achieving that desired outcome either through a "group-based, teacher-paced" approach or through an "individual-based and learner-paced" approach. Research on the mastery approach has enabled three major generalizations to be derived:

— Mastery learning is "effective";
— The key to its effectiveness lies within the feedback/corrective mechanism; and
— Mastery learning is differentially effective for different types of students, with lower ability and older students benefiting more than others.

In the final entry on models of teaching is *Heuristic Teaching Model*, that is, teaching designed to enhance problem solving and learners' ability to learn. One finds examples of concern with these matters as early as in Plato's writings and traces developments through the ages in the work of Aristotle, Quintilian, and others. Modern approaches are to be seen in the cognitive models of instruction of Montessori, Piaget, Bruner, Ausubel, Galperin, Wittrock, and Rogers.

References

Anderson, R.C. et. al. (1969): *Current Research on Instruction*, Prentice-Hall, Inc., Englewood Cliffs, New Jersy.

Bellack, A.A. (Ed.) (1963): *Theory and Research in Teaching*, Bureau of Publications, Teachers College, Columbia University, New York.

Bruner, J.S. (1966): *Toward A Theory of Instruction*, Harvard University Press, Cambridge, Mass.

Dunkin, M.J. (Ed.) (1987): *The International Encyclopaedia of Teaching and Teacher Education*, Pergamon Press, Oxford.

Flanders, N.A. (1965): Teacher Influence, Pupil Attitudes, and Achievement: *Studies in Interaction Analysis*, U.S. Office of Education, Co-operative Research Project No 397, Minneapolis, University of Minnesota.

Gage, N.L. et al. (1968): Exploration of the Teacher's Effectiveness in Explaining, *Technical Report No 4*, Stanford Centre for Research and Development in Teaching, Stanford University, U.S.A.

Glase, R. (Ed.) (1965): Teaching Machines and Programmed Learning, II Data and Directions, National Education Association, Department of Audio-Visual Instruction, Washington.

Jackson, P.W. (1966): "The Way Teaching is : Report of the Seminar on Teaching," Association for Supervision and Curriculum Development, National Education Association, Washington.

Joyce, B. and Weil, M. (1992): *Models of Teaching*, Prentice-Hall India, New Delhi, (4th ed.).

Skinner, B.F. (1959): "Teaching Machine," Science, 128.

Skinner, B.F. (1968): *The Technology of Teaching*, Appleton-Century Crofts, New York.

Smith, B.O. (1963): "Towards A Theory of Teaching," in Bellack, A.A. (Ed.) *Theory and Research in Teaching*, Bureau of Publications, Teachers College, Columbia University, New York.

Stolurow, L.M. (1965): "Model the Master Teacher or Master the Teaching Model," in Krumboltz, J. D. (Ed.), *Learning and the Educational Process*, Rand McNally and Co., Chicago.

Travers, R.W. (1966): "Towards Taking the Fun out of Building a Theory of Instruction," Teachers College Record, 68,49.

3.2 DESCRIPTION OF MODELS

3.2.1 Glaser: A Basic Teaching Model

Robert Glaser (1962) developed a basic psychological model of teaching. In this model the teaching process is divided into four components corresponding to the four major sequences of events in the instructional process. The components of the basic teaching model are depicted in Figure 3.2.1.

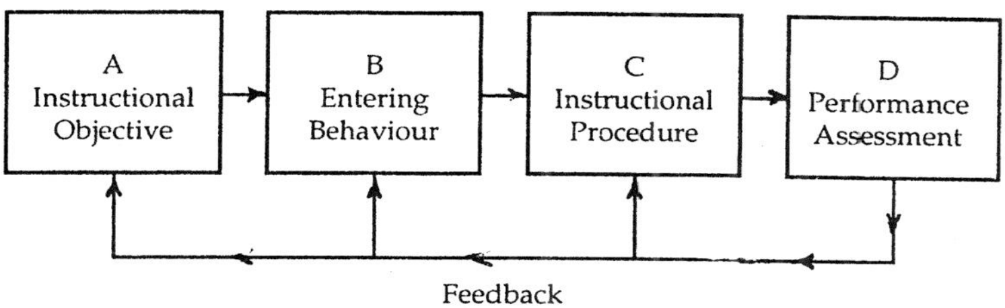

Fig. 3.2.1 Basic Teaching Model (Glaser, 1962)

In Box A is shown the instructional objectives which the students have to attain after the completion of the unit of instruction.

In Box B is shown the entering behaviour which indicates the students' level before instruction begins. It refers to the students' previous level of knowledge, his intellectual ability and development, his motivational state and certain social and cultural determinants of his learning abilities.

In Box C instructional procedure describes the teaching process itself. A teacher has to decide mostly on this procedure. Proper handling of this component will result in changes in students' behaviour such as learning or achievement.

Box D shows performance assessment. It contains test and observation which will determine how well the students have mastered the instructional objectives. After performance assessment the feed back will be given to C or B or A or any two or all the three of A, B, and C.

If it indicates that the achievement of the students is not up to the mark, then, all of the preceding components may require some sort of adjustment.

In this model, teacher's personality does not occupy a pivotal place, with the increasing use of technological devices the model puts a greater emphasis on teacher's competence and skills than on personal art of teaching.

References

DeCecco, J.P. and Crawford, W. (1977): *The Psychology of Learning and Instruction*, Prentice-Hall of India, New Delhi, (2nd ed.).

Glaser, R. (1962): "Psychology and Instructional Technology," in Glaser, R. (Ed.) *Training Research and Education*, University of Pittsburg Press, Pittsburg.

Instructional Entering Instructional Performance
Objective Behaviour Procedure Assessment

3.2.2 Herbart: Formal Steps in Teaching

Herbart was a philosopher and psychologist who developed an educational psychology based on the association of ideas. He made this work the starting point for a comprehensive study of perception and it became the basis for his proposals on educational method. Herbart attempted to act forth in a logical order the stages of systematic learning and formulated what are called Formal Steps in Teaching as a general guide to the class teacher. These are also known as the famous Herbartian steps.

Herbart developed a substantial theory of cognition centering on the process of apperception. A human mind consisted of ideas associated together in groups of related ideas. The first step in the process of learning was a contact with the outer world by sense-perception. This sensory impression was presented to ideas already within the mind and might be built into one of the existing groups. The process of fusing with an acceptable group and being related to the ideas within the group was called apperception. It was a vital part of the learning process not to\ be left to chance.

"Apperceptive mass" stands for the mind's existing store of ideas already lying in consciousness. This is the old stock of previously acquired ideas. All instruction is to be related to and harmonized with this old mass. Every new lesson in order to be effective and interesting must be connected with what the children already know. The instructor must make it a point to arouse the apperceptive mass of the pupils at the time of imparting new ideas. The educational problem thus becomes how to present new material in such a way that it can be apperceived or incorporated with the old.

The original formal steps of instruction, according to Herbart, were only four, viz. (i) clearness, (ii) association, (iii) assimilation and (iv) application. Later on, Herbart's disciple Ziller divided the step of clearness into two steps, viz., preparation and presentation. To guide teachers in their efforts, the Herbartians divided a series of instructional steps that became the most widely used aspect of Herbartian teaching method. The sequence differed slightly in nomenclature from time to time; its most popular form was in five steps: (a) preparation, (b) presentation, (c) association, (d) assimilation, and (e) application.

The teacher's task was, first, in preparation, to stir up in the pupil's mind the ideas upon which he wished to graft the new material in his lesson. He then presented his material, clearly, succinctly, and attractively, and proceeded to associate it with the ideas previously in the pupils mind, knitting it skillfully into the existing pattern.

The next step was to examine the fresh pattern formed out of the association of the new and old ideas. What was the meaning of the new apperception mass that had been formed?

The final step was that of fixing the new material in the pupils mind by applying it in a variety of ways, in tests, classroom exercises, and assignments for homework.

This sequence became a standard approach in the twentieth century for many subjects of the curriculum in primary and secondary schools in many countries. It was systematic, suitable for many different kinds of material, and was based on an easily comprehended theory of learning. In the hands of a skillful teacher it could be both thorough and intellectually exciting. The instructional sequence was associated with the "doctrine of interest."

When teaching became simply a matter of following the pattern of five formal steps with no concern for the psychological insight that had been put into the creation of them, or the interest and rich variation that a skilled Herbartian could develop in every aspect of them, they became a useful but somewhat "barren technique of instruction" and a refuge for conservative teachers seeking a well-tried routine. Herbartian method is only applicable to knowledge lesson and not for skill or appreciation lesson. Lastly, Herbart emphasised more on teaching rather than learning. However, interest was as important to the progressive educationists as to the Herbartians. "Interest", wrote Decorly, "is the sluice gate. By means of it the reservoir of attention is opened and directed."

Although Herbartian influence is still in practice for developing lesson plans, the Herbartians themselves have come out with certain criticisms. Human nature has been regarded as passive by Herbart and his followers, which is not true. The human child learns more by active manipulation and interaction with the environment than by passive listening and intermission as conceived in the Herbartian procedures. This procedure assumes convergence, conformity on the part of the students, in learning with a teacher who is dominant in the instructional process. Today's students look for divergence, flexibility and originality than a passive conformity. Learning for today's student is not fixed and stereotype. It is a process of change, improvement and discovery. In Herbartian system therefore, student's spontaneity is given low or no priority. The growing student thus becomes a uniform product than a unique product. Should instructional process be designed to cater to Herbartian steps any more?

Several alternative procedures of lesson planning and practice teaching are now obtained, of them, Davis (1981) model is a distinct improvement on yet comparable with Herbart's five formal steps, as shown in Table 3.2.1.

Table 3.2.1 Structure of a Basic Lesson for a 45 Minute Class

After Davis 1981				After Herbart 1904
Time in Mis.	Main Phase	Sub Phase	Typical Performance	Herbartian Steps
5	Introduction	Statement of Aim	Linkage Motivation Objectives	Preparation
		Development-1 (Examination Phase)	Attend Classify Label	Presentation
		Review-1	Recall	
	Development	Development-2 Interpretation Phase	Identify Explain Conclude	Comparison & Abstraction
		Review-2	Recall	
		Development-3 (Application Phase)	Practice (Encouragement correction)	Generalisation
35		Review-3	Recall	
	Consolidation	Revision of Whole	Retention of Whole	
		For Mastery	Reinforce Challenge Assess Mastery	Application
45		Any Question Next Lesson	Linkage	

Sample Format of Lesson Plan (in History)

Name of Institution	: Subject
Class	: Topic/Unit
Time	: Lesson Units and Sub-Units

I)INTRODUCTION (5 minutes)

i) Objectives	
a) General	: Complete learning of the lesson with attainment of desirable behaviours.
b) Specific	: To specify in behavioural terms the cognitive, psycho-motor and affective objectives relating to the lesson.
ii) Aids and appliances related to topic.	
iii) Preparation	: a) Questions and other activities based on previous knowledge to be linked with the day's lesson for motivating the students. b) Announcement of the lesson.

II) PRESENTATION (25 minutes):

	Teachers' Activity Method	*Students' Activity*
Matter Narration	a) Leading/Developmental questions	a) Answering questions
	b) B.B. Work	b) Proper use of aids and appliances
	c) Use of teaching aids and appliances.	c) To understand the lesson accurately and properly.

III) EVALUATION (10 minutes):

1) Asking questions for testing the assimilation of the days' lesson	1) Answering questions to reveal their assimilation.
2) Providing classroom exercises etc.	2) Performing classroom exercises etc. related to cognitive, psychomotor and affective level objective.

IV) ASSIGNMENT (5 minutes):
Assignment to be provided.

NOTE: This format is not at all rigid, it is flexible. It may change from lesson to lesson and topic to topic.

References

Dunkin. M.J. (Ed.) (1988): *The International Encyclopaedia of Teaching and Teacher Education*, Pergamon Press, Oxford.

Panda, K.C. (1991): "Lesson Planning," in Bhattacharya, S.P. (Ed.) *Teaching To Be* Learning Resources House, Calcutta.

3.2.3 Flanders: Interaction Analysis Model

Interaction analysis model views the dynamics of the classroom through a particular lens. What interaction analysis captures is the verbal behaviour of teachers and pupils that is directly related to the socio-emotional climate of the classroom. Interaction analysis as a classroom observational technique was developed by Ned A Flanders out of socio-physchological theory and was designed to test the effect of socio-emotional climate on students' attitude and learning.

Flanders concerned himself with the verbal statements of teachers as they occur in the spontaneous interaction of the classroom. He developed a technique of recording and analyzing the data. The purpose he mentioned as:

> "A theory of teacher influence, or, more modestly, some hypothesis of teacher influence will be developed and tested."

Flanders observed, the ultimate goal of the study of teacher influence in the classroom was to achieve understanding of teacher-pupil interaction, and, in particular to specify conditions in which learning will be maximized.

Flanders classified teacher influence as 'Direct', when a teacher sets restraints upon a student or focusses students' attention upon an idea, and 'Indirect', when he reduces a restraint upon students and encourages students' participation. In interaction analysis of Flanders is used a 3 second interval time-sampling observation technique for coding the type of teacher-pupil talks in 10 categories. By sampling about every 3 seconds, the observer will have made about 400 entries in 20 minutes. The pattern of teacher behaviour can be viewed by the frequency as well as the patterning of categories. Flanders used 10 categories, 7 assigned to teachers' talk and 2 to students' talk and 1 to silence or confusion. The categories are given in Table 3.2.2.

Flanders' study has shown that, by and large, students in classes with higher Indirect/Direct ratio achieve more and possess better attitude than students with lower Indirect/Direct ratio. His work has made a fundamental contribution towards a model of teaching, identifying general patterns of teachers'

Table 3.2.2 Flanders' Interaction Analysis Category System

Teacher Talk	Indirect	1. Accepts Feelings 2. Praises or Encourages 3. Accepts or Uses Ideas of Students 4. Asks Questions
	Direct	5. Lecturing 6. Giving Direction 7. Criticizes or Justifies Authority
Student Talk		8. Student Talk: Response 9. Student Talk: Initiation
		10. Silence or Confusion

influence that produce predictable pupils' response. Flanders has identified some critical teaching behaviour which he found on the basis of statistical analysis of his 10-category data. He defines a critical teaching behaviour as a pattern of acts that: (a) are logically related to certain instructional outcomes; (b) follow a certain sequence with measurable probability and (c) seem crucial in terms of a theory of teacher influence verified by earlier research.

Flanders (1960) states the three principles of teacher influence to which the interaction model applies.

Restricting students' freedom of participation early in the cycle of classroom learning activities increases dependence and decreases achievement.

Restricting students' freedom of participation later in the cycle of classroom learning activities does not increase dependence but does increase achievement.

Expanding students' freedom of participation early in the cycle of classroom learning activities decreases dependence and increases achievement.

The teacher restricts students' freedom of participation when he exercises direct influence (categories 5, 6 and 7 in Table 3.2.2) through lecturing, giving directions, and criticizing or justifying authority. In these behaviour categories the teacher talks more, and therefore plays a dominant role in the classroom. Expansion of student participation occurs, when the teacher employs categories 1 through 4. The teacher accepts feeling, praises or encourages, accepts or uses students' ideas, and asks questions.

In short, Flanders' research on classroom interaction has added a new prospect toward building a model of teaching.

Reference

DeCecco, J.P. & Crawford, W. (1977): The *Psychology of Learning and Instruction: Educational Psychology*, Prentice-Hall of India, New Delhi (2nd edn.) pp. 13-16.

Flanders, N.A. (1960): *Teacher Influence, Pupil Attitudes, and Achievement*, Univ. of Minnesota, Minneapolis.

3.2.4 Bruner: Concept Attainment Model (CAM)

The Concept Attainment Model (CAM) of teaching has been presented by Bruner, Goodnow and Austin (Figure 3.2.2). It is developed from their study of Thinking (1977). The Concept Attainment Strategy as model of teaching is concerned with two separate but related ideas:

— nature of the concepts themselves; and
— thinking process used by individual to learn concepts.

Nature of Concepts

Concepts are the basic building blocks for the structure of knowledge of an academic discipline (e.g. physics, economics, botany, etc.). They are the distillate of sensory experiences and the vital link between external inputs and overt behaviour. They are the critical components of an individual's cognitive structure.

A concept is assumed to be a set of specific objects or events, which share common characteristics, and they can be referred to by a particular name.

Concept learning is thus regarded as the identification of concept attributes which can be generalised to newly encountered examples and discriminate examples from non-examples.

Thinking Strategies of Concept Attainment

Bruner analyses any concept as having five elements.

i) *Name*—It is a term given to the category
ii) *Examples*—They refer to the instances of the concept. Examples of a concept may be positive or negative.
iii) *Attributes*—The basic characteristics of the concepts are called attributes. Each attribute has an attribute value.
iv) *Attribute Value*—This refers to the specific content of that category of concept. Most attributes have a range of accepted value.
v) *The rule* is a definition or statement of specifying the essential attributes of a concept.

Suppose there is an array of fruits in front of you, mostly apples but one or two oranges and a pear. Each fruit is an example or instance. If my concept is 'apple' the pears and oranges are negative instances and the apples are positive instances. Each example can be described in terms of the basic characteristics. In the case of fruit, these are colour, size, weight, shape and costs. These basic characteristics are called attributes and each attribute has an attribute value. The term 'attribute value' refers to the specific content of that category (in this case yellow or red). Most attributes have a range of acceptable values. The attribute value for an apple is arranged from red to yellow. Purple is out of the acceptable value range of the concept "apple".

Now the elements of a concept, particularly attributes and examples, play important roles in students' thought process, directed to concept attainment.

Bruner and the associates identified regularities in students' decision-making processes that they labelled thinking strategies. On the basis of their research they developed concept attainment teaching strategies of two types:

i) Selection strategies: Here teacher presents unlabelled examples of the concept and the student chooses concept instances. The selection strategies place responsibility for concept attainment and attribute tracking in the hands of the students.
ii) Reception strategies: The teacher presents examples of the concept that are labelled 'Yes' or 'No' and students hypothesize the concept and accept or reject an example.

The 'Concept Attainment Model' developed by Bruner and his associates have three variations:

a) *Reception Model* is more direct in teaching students the elements of a concept and their use in concept attainment.
b) *Selection Model* permits students to apply this awareness of conceptual activity in a more active context, one that permits their own initiation and control.
c) *Unorganised Material Model*: The analysis of concepts in unorganised data transfers concept theory and attainment activity to a real life setting.

Illustration of the Model (From the Reception Strategy)

A primary school teacher decides to teach a concept 'Domestic Animals' to 5th Graders. She begins the activity by saying that she has a category in mind and she is going to present certain examples that fit into that category and certain non-examples

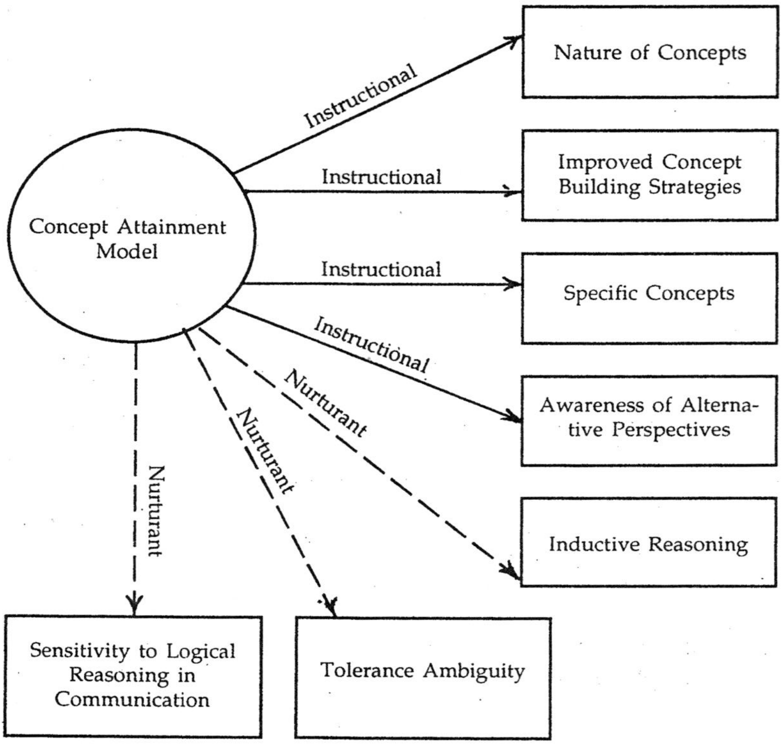

Fig. 3.2.2 Instructional and Nurturant Effect: Concept Attainment Model

that do not fit into the category. The positive examples are denoted by 'Yes' and negative examples are denoted by 'No'. Then the teacher writes on the blackboard the following examples and asks the pupil to determine the category.

	eg. 1		Cow—'Yes'.
			Tiger—'No'.
Student	ST A	—	It is an animal that gives us milk.
	ST B	—	Whose meat is not eaten by Hindus.
	ST C	—	An animal which is worshipped by Hindus.
	ST D	—	An animal that people keep in their houses.
	eg. 2		Goat—'Yes'.
	ST E	—	The category is an animal that gives milk.

The example of goat has now forced the learners to eliminate the earlier two hypotheses—the animal is not eaten by Hindus; and the animal which is not worshipped by Hindus.

Teacher — Let us go a bit further. She presents one more example and asks the learners to test their hypothesis in the light of this datum.

eg. 3 Dog—'Yes'.

ST F — It can't be an animal which gives us milk. The concept is simply an animal.

Teacher — Let us continue and present another example.

eg. 4 Lion—'No'.

ST G — It is not an animal which people keep in their houses.

Teacher — Presents two more examples.

eg. 5 Horse—'Yes'

eg. 6 Monkey—'No'

ST H — The concept is an animal which people keep in their houses for their use.

Teacher — What precise name we can give to this concept? After having no or partial response, the teacher tells the learner that the concept is 'Domestic Animal.' Domestic animals are those, which are reared by man for his own use or pleasure. The teacher then suggests, 'Let us look at all the positive examples and determine the attributes/characteristics they have in common.'

ST I — They are reared by man.

ST J — They are used by man for his use or pleasure. The teacher asks the pupil to suggest some positive examples.

ST K — 'Pig'.

ST L — 'Buffalo'.

Teacher—Children we have learnt today as to what is meant by 'Domestic Animals'.

The Concept Attainment Models are appropriate for several educational objectives. They can be used to:

1. Help students acquire a new concept;
2. Enrich and clarify their thinking on previously acquired concepts;
3. Teach them 'the concept of a concept,' including the terminology and meaning of a concept theory and conceptual activity; and
4. Help them become aware of their own thinking processes and strategies.

References

Bruner, J., Goodnow, J.J. & Austin, G.A. (1967): *A Study of Thinking*, Science Editions, Inc., New York.

Joyce, B. and Weil, M. (1992): *Models of Teaching*, Prentice-Hall of India, New Delhi.

3.2.5 Suchman: Inquiry Training Model (ITM)

The Inquiry Training Model was developed by Richard Suchman. Inquiry training begins with a puzzling event. Suchman believes that individuals, faced with a puzzling situation, are motivated to pursue the meaning in it. They naturally seek to understand what they encounter. In order to understand puzzling situations, they must increase the complexity of their thinking and understand better how to link data into concepts and how to apply those concepts towards the identification of principles of causation. Thus the underlying assumption of the model is that individuals, when puzzled, need to explore the data surrounding the puzzlement and put these data together in new ways. They inquire and as they inquire, they recognise their knowledge.

According to him, the students can become more and more conscious of the process of inquiry, and that this process can be taught to them directly. He sees conscious awareness of the process and strategies of inquiry as an essential aspect of autonomous inquiry. Suchman feels we cannot analyse and improve our thinking, unless we are consciously aware of it.

Suchman deliberately selects episodes that have sufficiently surprising outcomes to make it difficult for students to remain indifferent to the encounter. (The problem is obviously based on content in the syllabus of a school subject.) The learners cannot dismiss the solution as obvious; they have to work to explain the situation, and the product of that work is a new insight into the phenomenon, new concepts, new theories.

A unique feature of this model lies in the fact that, the teacher structures the situation in such a way that the questions must be answerable by a 'yes' or a 'no'. This eliminates open-ended questions. Students may not ask the teacher to explain the phenomenon to them. They have to focus and structure their probes in order to solve the problem. The teacher may guide the students to a strategy whereby their earlier questions are confined to analysing and verifying the situation they have observed—trying to find out the nature and identify the object, the events, and the conditions surrounding the puzzling situation.

The goals of Inquiry Training are to help students develop the intellectual discipline necessary to search out data, process it, and apply logic to it. Suchman is interested in helping students to inquire independently, but in a disciplined way. Sheer independent learning is not his goal. He wants students to question why events happen as they do, and to develop intellectual strategies that they can use to determine casual relationships among phenomena.

To make it clear as to how the inquiry cycle begins we can cite a concrete example.

A teacher is interested in teaching the students of Class V the essential conditions for the growth of a tree. So he/she has formulated a puzzling problem for them and presented the problem thus:

Teacher: Your school has a small nursery. Ramu is a gardener in your school. He has been growing plants in the school nursery for many years. This year also he planted seeds of peas in a small plot of the nursery. He nurtured the plants as usual and he noted that seedlings came out. After sometime he observed that the plants turned pale and started dying.

After posing the above mentioned problem the teacher wanted the students to find out the reason why the plants turned pale and started dying.

Pupil (1) — Sir, was the soil fit for growing plants?
Teacher (T) — Yes.
P(2) — Did Ramu plough the plot properly?
T — Yes
P(1) — Was the soil free from stones?
T — Yes.
P(2) — Were the seeds used of good quality?
T — Yes.
P(2) — Did Ramu give water to the plot regularly.
T — Yes.
P(3) — Has the plot become deficient in certain minerals because of its use over the years?
T — No
P(3) — Did Ramu add appropriate fertilizers to the plot?
T — Yes.
P(3) — Was the soil treated with insecticide?
T — Yes.
P(3) — Did Ramu provide either inadequate or too much water to the plants?

T — No.
P(4) — Was it affecting the growth of the plants?
T — Yes.
P(3) — Sir, I am sure that the plants turned pale and started dying as they were not getting adequate sunlight.
Teacher — Yes, Mohan, very good. You have identified the reason for the plants getting pale and dying. What do you infer from this problem?
Mohan — Sir, 'sunlight' is essential for the growth of plants.
Teacher — So, well prepared soil, manure and fertilizers, insecticides, minerals, good seed, water and also sunlight are essential for proper growth of plants.

So for establishing an environmental fact illustrated above, the teacher, with the help of the students, has followed several steps which are:

1. *Encounter with the Problem*

This is a step where presentation of the puzzling problem is done by the teacher. Before presentation, the teacher selected a topic or problem which is challenging, motivating and suitable for developing inquiry skills among the students.

2. *Data Gathering (Exploration)*

The students discuss within themselves, and with the teacher; and above all from their memory, they collect the required data essential for formulating the possible explanation of the given problem. In this step teacher directs the students to organise their knowledge for explaining and establishing cause and effect relationship.

3. *Data Gathering (Experimentation)*

The process of data collection continues in this step also like in step-2 with the only difference that here the students formulate some hypothesis (explanation), test them, try to verify it with cause-effect relationship, isolate the non-relevant variables or factors, and if situation demands, they can reject the hypothesis also, re-establishing a fresh one.

4. *Formulating an Explanation*

On the basis of step (3), the explanation of the posed problem is established and declared by the teacher.

5. *Analysis of the Inquiry Process*

Every inquiry process has its strength and weakness. The students have to ask themselves whether the approach adopted by them was the only one feasible or they had a multiple choice. In the latter case the question is whether the other choice(s) could help in searching out more effective ways of inquiry. Unfortunately this step was not covered in the teaching episode.

The whole process undertaken in the inquiry training model can be represented in the following steps:

Hypothesis Formed	⇒	Data Gathered	⇒	Data Support Hypothesis	⇒	Hypothesis Retained
Alternate Hypothesis	⇒	Data Gathered	⇒	Data do not Support Hypothesis	⇒	Hypothesis Rejected

Uses of the Model

1. It promotes autonomous learning as students are engaged in formulating the questions and testing the ideas.
2. By using this model self-learning and individual inquiry skills of the students are promoted.
3. The group discussion helps students to establish a very good friendship among themselves.
4. It also strengthens the verbal expressions and vocabularies of the students.

This model can be used for all types of students right from Kindergarden children to higher secondary students. It was originally devised for reading natural science subjects but the procedure can be strongly used in other subjects also.

The emphasis in this model is clearly on becoming aware of and mastering the inquiry process, not on the content and explanation of any particular problem situation. Although the model should also be enormously appealing and effective as a mode of acquiring and using information, the teacher cannot be too concerned with subject matter coverage or 'correctness.' In fact, this would violate the whole spirit of scientific inquiry, which envisions a community of scholars searching together for more accurate and powerful explanations for everyday phenomena.

The Instructional (direct) and Nurturant (indirect) Effects of Inquiry Training Model are given in Figure 3.2.3.

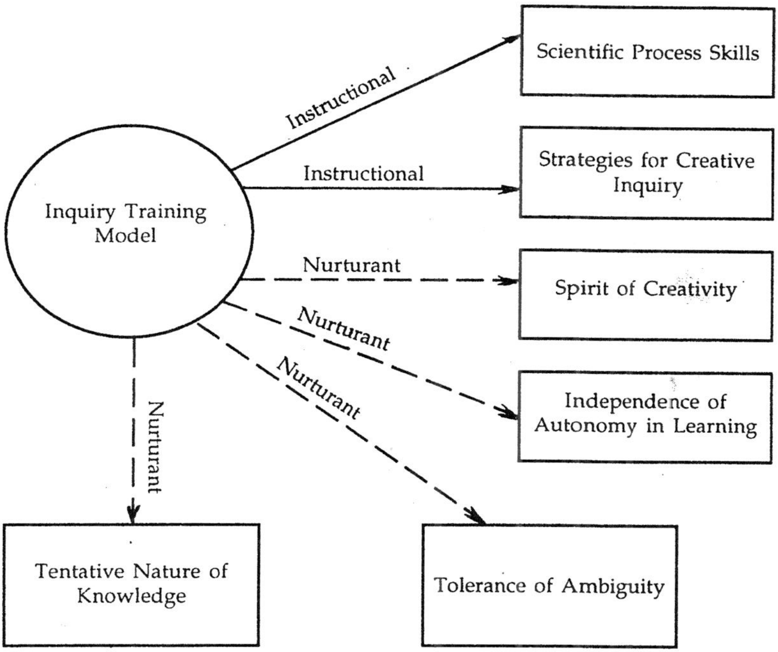

Fig. 3.2.3 Instructional (direct) and Nurturant (Indirect) Effects of Inquiry Training Model

References

Joyce, B. and Weil, M. (1992): *Models of Teaching*, Prentice-Hall of India, New Delhi.

Suchman, R.J. (1964): "Studies in inquiry training," in R. Ripple and V. Bookcastle (Eds.), *Piaget Reconsidered*, Cornell University Press, Ithaca, N.Y.

3.2.6 Ausubel: Advance Organiser Model (AOM)

Ausubel, in his 'Theory of Meaningful Learning' advocates the use of advance organisers to facilitate the learning of written material (Figure 3.2.4). The theory deals with three concerns:

i) How is knowledge organised? (curriculum content)
ii) How does the mind work to process new information? (learning)
iii) How can these ideas about curriculum and learning be applied by teachers, when they present new material to students? (instruction)

Ausubel's primary concern is to help teachers convey large amounts of information as meaningfully and efficiently as possible. He believes that the acquisition of information is a valid, indeed an essential goal of schooling and there are theories that can guide teachers in their job of transmitting bodies of knowledge to their students. His own ideas of how this learning takes place is embodied in this "Theory of Meaningful Verbal Learning" (1963).

According to Ausubel, 'Meaningful learning' implies that what we have learnt is intellectually linked and understood in

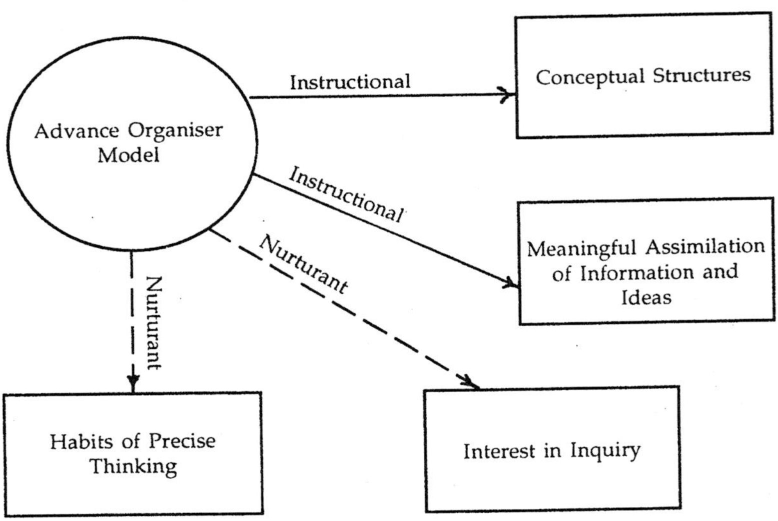

Fig. 3.2.4 Instructional and Nurturant Affects of Advance Organiser Model

the context or what we previously knew. It also implies that we can transform this knowledge and apply it creatively in new and rather novel situations. He says, whether the material is meaningful depends on the learner and the material, not the method of presentation. If the learner employs a meaningful learning set, and if the material is potentially meaningful for the student, then meaningful learning can occur.

This theory applies to situations where the teacher plays the role of lecturer or explainer. Characteristically, the teacher presents the entire content of what is to be learnt directly to the learner. The learner's primary role is that of recipient of ideas and information and ultimately to internalize the material.

The advance organiser model is designed to strengthen students' cognitive structures. By cognitive structure, Ausubel means a person's knowledge of a particular subject matter at any given time and how well organised, clear and stable it is.

He maintains that a person's existing 'cognitive structure' is the foremost factor governing whether new material is potentially meaningful and how well it can be acquired and retained. Strengthening students' retention of new information is one of the model's primary goal.

In regard to the 'structure of a discipline', Ausubel believes that there is a parallel between the way subject matter is organised and the way people organise knowledge in their minds (their cognitive structure). He opines that each of the academic disciplines has a structure of concepts or propositions that are organised hierarchically. That is, at the top of each discipline are a number of very broad concepts that include or subsume the inclusive concepts at lower stages of information. Ausubel conceptualizes a discipline as level of these hierarchically organised concepts that begin with perceptual data at the bottom and proceed through increasing levels of abstraction to the most abstract concepts at the top.

In the actual teaching situation, the primary way of strengthening cognitive structure and enhancing retention of new information is through the use of advance organisers. Ausubel describes *Advance Organisers* in the following way: "An Advance Organiser is introductory material that is presented ahead of the learning task and is at a higher level of abstraction and inclusiveness than the learning task itself. Its purpose is to explain, integrate, and interrelate the material in the learning task with previously learned material. Advance Organisers are generally based upon the major concepts, propositions, generalisations, principles and laws of a discipline, that are already familiar to the learner." For example, a lesson or text describing the caste system in India might be preceded by an organiser based on the concept of social stratification.

Time must be taken to explain and develop the organiser, for only when it is fully understood, it can serve to organise the subsequent learning material. For example, the students must fully understand the concept of culture before it can be effectively used to organise factual information about different culture groups.

Advance organisers, are of two types:

— Expository
— Comparative

Expository Organisers provide a general model of class relationship as a general subsumer for a new class, subclasses, and species before more limited subsumers (classes) are provided for the particular subclass or species. For example, before discussing specific types of mechanical energy, such as potential and kinetic, an instructor would build an expository organiser around the concept of mechanical energy, describing what it is and how it functions and providing several examples. These organisers are especially helpful because they provide ideational scaffolding for unfamiliar materials.

Comparative Organisers, on the other hand, are used most with relatively familiar material. They are organised to integrate new concepts with basically similar concepts existing in the cognitive structure; they also discriminate between the old and the new concepts in order to prevent confusion caused by their similarity. For example, when the learner is being introduced to long division, a comparative organiser might be used that would stress the similarity and yet the differences of division facts and multiplication facts.

There are *three phases* of activity in the Advance Organiser Model.

The *first phase* consists of three activities; clarifying the aims of the lesson, presenting the advance organiser, and promoting awareness of relevant knowledge and experience.

Phase *two* is the presentation of the learning task or learning materials.

The last phase or *phase three* draws students into a more overt though not necessarily intellectually more active role. It tests the relationship of the learning material to existing cognitive organisation and induces active reception learning.

The effectiveness of the model depends on the conceptual organiser and the content.

Uses

a) This model is useful to instruct students systematically in the key ideas of a field of knowledge;
b) It increases the learner's grasp of factual information;
c) Whenever ideas or informations need to be presented, renewed or clarified, the advance organiser is a useful model; and
d) The model nurtures an interest in inquiry—a precise habit of thinking.

References

Ausubel, D.P. (1977): *Behaviour Modification for the Classroom Teacher*, McGraw-Hill, New York.

Joyce, B. and Weil, M. (1992): *Models of Teaching*, Prentice-Hall of India, New Delhi.

3.2.7 Piaget: Cognitive Growth Model (Increasing the capacity to think)

The noted Swiss psychologist Jean Piaget has devoted himself since 1920 to the study of the development of intellectual processes. Based on his work, American psychologists like Lawrence Kohlberg and Irving Siegel have crafted teaching methods designed to improve intellectual development in general and moral development in particular.

Piaget's studies of intellectual development find their applications to education. His views include organisation of the educational environment, curriculum content and sequence, methods of teaching and assessment. The role of a teacher is not clearly prescribed anywhere. Some say it is the teacher who matches the curriculum to the student's stage of development. Others are of opinion that the teacher accelerates intellectual development of the student. The model of teaching based on Piaget's philosophy is for assessing the learner's stage of the development. To know the model of teaching we have to follow different research works of Flaveu, Hunt, Furth, Siegel and Hooper and Wadsworth.

Piaget classified intellectual development into different stages (Figure 3.2.5). At any given stage one is able to perform certain kinds of thinking. The earlier stages lay the basis for future development. The stages are:

1. Sensorimotor stage (0 to 2 yrs.)
2. Pre-operational stage (2 to 7 yrs.)
   a) Preconceptual stage (2 to 4 yrs.)
   b) Intuitive thought (4 to 7 yrs.)
3. Operational stage (7 to 16 yrs.)
   a) Concrete operational thought (7 to 11 yrs.)
   b) Formal operational thought (11 to 16 yrs.)

Principles of Learning and Teaching

1. Wadsworth summarised Piaget's ideas on teaching and learning. According to him teaching is the creation of environment where the student's congnitive structure can emerge and change. In a suitable environment students will obviously initiate their own learning experiences and in that case

their cognitive structures will grow and the learning will be spontaneous. Here the student's role is active and self-discovering. The teacher's function is to arrange for learning experiences that facilitate stage-relevant thinking and to organise instruction so that students can initiate the activity and discover for themselves.

2. The second principle is based on Piaget's distinction among three types of knowledge: Physical, Social and Logical. The nature of matter (softness, hardness etc.) gives the physical knowledge. Social knowledge comes from society in which a student lives. It originates from various social actions and social connections. Logical knowledge is mostly related to mathematics and logic.
3. The last principle of teaching and learning deals with the role of the social environment.

Based on these three principles the roles of teacher can be specified as:

i) Organiser of the learning environment;
ii) Assessor of children's thinking; and
iii) Initiator of group activities like play, games, discussions etc.

During past ten years several models of teaching have been developed. First model is formulated by Celia Lavatelle and meant for children from four to seven years old. The objective of this method is to develop children's intellectual ability through self-directed activity. It consists of 100 activities occurring over a thirty week period. These activities are to be finished in 10-15 minutes with small groups of five to six children.

Second model was done by Waikart in his 'Programmes Project Follow Through': He focusses on socio-emotional development as well as cognitive.

Third model is depicted by Kamil and Devries. According to them a child must learn to construct his/her own knowledge provided a teacher through appropriate questions and suggestions facilitates this process. They stressed on the importance of children's play as a learning medium and suggested some sets of games.

Further Olson and Siegel gave their own models where they suggested alternative instructional approaches to help the students to think at a higher level.

It is clear from all the researches that a good teacher has to undertake constant and continuous assessing process. Piaget describes such a process as 'method clinique' (the clinical method).

The model, described below, is based on the principles of clinical interview designed by Piaget. Before we go into the model proper let us briefly sketch Piaget's clinical method.

Pieget's dissatisfactions with pure observations and with the validity of the most standardised testing led him to observe that the skill of the practitioner consists not in making the child answer questions but in making him talk freely and thus engaging the flow of his spontaneous tendency instead of diverting it into the artificial channels of set questions and answers. He refers to this procedure as the clinical interview, the goal of which is to ascertain the nature or stage of the child's reasoning by "testing the limits" of the child's capabilities. In a one-to-one situation, a child is given a task typically designed to assess one area of thinking. The interviewer then asks questions, and as the child responds, he or she listens to and observes the child's behaviour. Based on a hypothesis about the level of thinking, more questions are asked until the interviewer is convinced that requirements for the level of thinking have been met. In this situation both wrong and right answers are useful. However, the interviewer must be careful not to pre-determine the child's responses by formulating questions which will provide a clue to the child. Piaget observes that all the students' responses during the clinical interview may not be equally useful. The students may be uninterested in the question at that moment, they may give an answer they really do not believe or they may respond to an implied suggestion given by the interviewer. The most valued reflections are those based on conviction given either after reflection or spontaneously. The important way of segregating useful from worthless answers is to make counter suggestions and also by probing the student's answers to ascertain how deep-rooted those are. Another way is to let the student talk for a while and then ask the question again in several different guises. If a student is at a specific reasoning level, he or she can make a correct judgement, offer a logical justification to the judgement, successfully resist a verbal counter-suggestion and complete a successful performance on a related task.

Based on the principles of clinical interview we shall now develop the model of teaching. The model requires teachers to give tasks, observe how the students interact with the tasks, and then respond in accordance with the students' actions, say by asking for justification or offering counter suggestions. After making his or her assessment of the students' performance either individually or in a group, the teacher must determine the general range of development stages of the students so as to avoid inappropriate tasks being included in the curriculum.

Syntax

The model has three phases, as indicated in the Table on next page. In the first phase, the students are presented with a situation which may be puzzling to them as that may confront them with the illogic of their thinking. However, confronting situation must be well matched to the learners' developmental stage. Also, the confronting situation should be such as to permit the students to assimilate on the strength of the prior learning but it should be new enough to require accommodation.

In phase two, the students' responses are called for and their level of reasoning is determined through probing, which generally will consist of asking for justification or offering counter suggestions. To start with, depending on the type of task, the teacher may start with question like "What do you think?" or "What do you see?" The need for probing is an attempt to obtain the correct response, if there is a correct response. Next the student is asked to justify the response by indicating his or her reasoning. After the reasoning is persuaded, one or more counter suggestions may be made in order to verify the soundness of a student's reasoning.

Syntax of Developmental Model

Phase One Confrontation with Stage-relevant Task	Phase Two Enquiry	Phase Three Transfer
Present puzzling situation well matched to learner's developmental stage.	Elicit student responses and ask for justification, offer counter-suggestions, probe student's responses.	Present related task and probe student's reasoning. Offer counter-suggestions.

Phase three i.e. the transfer phase has the objectives of seeing whether the student's reasoning will be similar for a related task. Here also the students are given a problem, they make judgements. The teacher requests for reasoning and offer counter-suggestions.

Social System

The social system can range from minimally structured to highly structured. However, a fairly structural teaching model with the teacher initiating and guiding the enquiry in a free intellectual and social atmosphere may be more suitable.

Principles of Reaction

The teacher must create an environment where the students will feel like responding spontaneously, and at the same time he or she should carefully avoid cuing questions. He or she has to enquire into both 'wrong' and 'correct' responses. He or she also should constantly check students' thinking with counter-suggestions, until he or she is satisfied that the students have attained the particular level of reasoning.

Support System

It is desirable that a teacher is quite knowledgeable in developmental theory. He or she must also have adequate stock of relevant counter-suggestions for Piagetian educational models. A rich resource environment as well as a free social environment that permits students to work out the cognitive problems are essentially required. In such a situation a useful role for the teacher will be in the form of a facilitator offering appropriate comments at the right moment.

Application

This model has applicability to both cognitive and social development. In fact, it can be used in areas confronted with illogic or problems in thinking and also for diagnosis and evaluation and for instructional purposes. The model can be employed to ensure that a child can operate smoothly in his or her environment or to find out activities that will accelerate the child's cognitive growth.

After Piaget another remarkable research on moral development of the child was done by Kohlberg. He identifies three major levels of moral development—pre-conventional, conventional, and post-conventional. Each level has two stages.

According to Kohlberg it is possible to influence child's level of thinking and for this a well guided, organised instruction is to be formulated in accordance with the various developmental stages. But matching teaching to moral levels is not a very easy task. To provide a stage-four task to a stage-one child is not productive. Teaching should be one level higher than the student's level of functioning. Kohlberg's thesis is very clear and very promising.

Instructional and Nurturant Effects of Developmental Model

The effects of any model of teaching can be categorized as (a) the direct or instructional effects which are those directly achieved by leading the learner in certain directions; and (b) the nurturant effects that come from experiencing the environment created by the model.

To bring a change in the cognitive development following Piaget's model, it is necessary to affect all aspects of functioning. Thus one aspect of cognition will nurture development in all other areas.

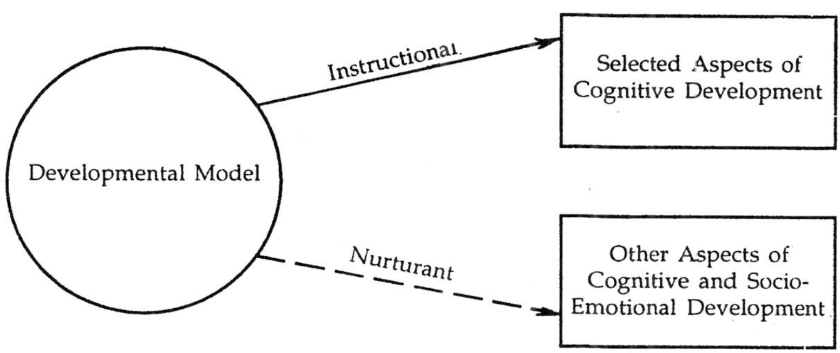

Fig. 3.2.5 Instructional and Nurturant Effects of Development Model

References

Joyce, B. and Weil, M. (1992): *Models of Teaching*, Prentice-Hall of India, New Delhi.

Piaget, J. (1952): The *Origins of Intelligence in Children*, International University Press, New York.

3.2.8 Gagne: The Conditions of Learning: Focussing Instruction

An important contribution in the field of learning and teaching has been made by Robert N. Gagne in his book entitled *Conditions of Learning* (1965). Though he has not provided a model of teaching as such, he has given a careful analysis of the key variables in learning and how instruction can be organised to take these variables into account. He speaks of six varieties of performances which may result from learning. These are:

i) Specific responding
ii) Chaining
iii) Multiple discrimination
iv) Classifying
v) Rule using
vi) Problem solving

By *specific responding* Gagne means a specific response to a particular stimulus. For example, when a teacher in the first grade shows a card with the word 'dog' printed on it, the children say 'dog'. Specific responding is an extremely important type of learning and is the basis for much of the informations we possess.

Chaining is making a series of responses that are linked together. Examples are unlocking a door with a key and translating from one language to another.

Multiple discrimination involves learning a variety of specific responses and chains and how to sort them out appropriately. For example, we learn to associate colours with varieties of objectives under different conditions choosing the right response and chain.

Classifying involves assigning objects to classes denoting like functions. We learn to distinguish plants from animals or automobiles from bicycles.

A *rule using* is an ability to act on a concept that implies action. For example, in spelling one learns varieties of concepts which describe how words are spelt. Then one applies these concepts in a rule form to the act of spelling.

Finally, *problem solving* is the application of several rules to a problem not encountered earlier by the learner. Problem solving requires selecting the correct rules and applying them in combination.

Gagne feels that these classes of learning have an ascending hierarchy. Thus we have to learn specific responses before we can learn chaining, or multiple discrimination will require prior learning of several chains in their independent form. Again only when we learn multiple discrimination we can develop classification. Rules for action can be built up through classification and the establishment of casual relations. For problem solving one requires previously learned rules. Each level of learning presupposes certain conditions, and the task of the instructor is to provide these conditions by using the appropriate model of teaching.

Gagne stresses the fact that though it is the learner's activity that results in the learning, it is the function of the instructor to provide *conditions* that will facilitate the students to attain a particular level of performance. Through practice the learner makes the necessary connections even when these are pointed out to him. The instructor can not substitute his or her activity for the activity of the students.

The instructional system operates through the following instructional functions:

i) Informing the learner of the objectives
ii) Presenting stimuli
iii) Increasing learner's attention
iv) Helping the learner recall what he or she has previously learnt
v) Providing conditions that will evoke performance
vi) Determining sequence of learning
vii) Prompting and guiding the learning.

The instructor also encourages the students to generalise that they are learning so that the new skills and knowledge may be transferred into other situations.

Gagne has given an instructional paradigm which is quite useful in defining the learning outcomes and the objectives of instruction. Models of teaching especially from the information processing and cybernatic/behaviour modification families may be effectively used to design many of these conditions.

Though Gagne's instructional paradigm may appear to be very direct and highly controlling, he stresses the fact that we can not control learning but can only enhance the probability that certain kinds of behaviour may occur. Certain kinds of stimuli in connection with others may be presented and students may be asked to perform but it is the learner who is to establish the connection between what is printed and what is spoken.

From this angle, a model of teaching brings to the students' environment such change, in the probability that he or she will learn certain things. More complex models involve activities likely to increase the probability of several kinds of learning taking place. Gagne's hierarchy is useful in helping us select models appropriate for varieties of educational objectives.

References:

Joyce, B. and Weil, M. (1992): *Models of Teaching*, Prentice-Hall of India, New Delhi.

Gagne, R. (1967): Instruction in the conditions of learning, in Laurence Siegel (Ed.), *Instruction: Some Contemporary Viewpoints*, Harper & Row, New York.

3.2.9 Carroll: Mastery Learning Model of Teaching

According to Carroll (1963), if the students are normally distributed with respect to aptitude for some subject and all the students are provided with exactly the same instruction (same in terms of amount and quality of instruction and time available for learning), the end result will be a normal distribution as an appropriate measure of achievement. Furthermore, the relation between aptitude and achievement will be fairly high (a correlation of + 0.7 or higher is to be expected, if the aptitude and achievement measures are valid and reliable). Conversely, if the students are normally distributed with respect to aptitude but the kind and quality of instruction and the amount of time available for learning are made appropriate to the characteristics and needs of each learner, the majority of students may be expected to achieve mastery of the subject. And the relation between aptitude and achievement should approach zero. It is this basic set of ideas Carroll developed in his model.

Teachers have come to recognise that individuals do differ in their aptitudes in particular kinds of learning, and therefore the students with high levels of aptitude can learn the complex ideas of the subject while the students with low levels of aptitude can learn only the simplest ideas of the subject. Quite in contrast to this is Carroll's view that aptitude is the amount of time required by the learner to attain mastery in a learning task. According to Bloom (1971) given sufficient time and appropriate types of help, 95 percent of students can achieve Grade A as an index of mastery of a subject.

First problem is to determine how individual differences in learners can be related to variations in the quality of instruction. Given help and various types of aids, individual teachers can find ways of modifying their instruction to match the differing needs of their students. One way is to vary the instructional materials like text books, work books and programmed instruction units, learning package, audio visual methods and academic games.

Throughout the world, schools are organised to give group instruction with definite periods of time allocated for particular learning tasks. According to Carroll, the time spent on learning is the key to mastery. His basic assumption is that aptitude determines the rate of learning and that all students can achieve mastery, if they devote the amount of time needed to the learning.

The central strategy for mastery, 'learning is the development of feedback and corrective procedures at various stages of learning process.' It is found that the development of brief diagnostic-progress tests proved to be most useful. Such tests are intended to determine what each student has learned in a particular unit and what he still needs to learn. In general these formative tests are not used to grade or judge the student, but are of value in providing feedback to both the teacher and the learner on what aspects or elements of the learning unit are still needed to be mastered. The diagnosis should be accompanied by a very specific prescription, if the students are to do anything about it.

The results of a strategy for mastery learning has two facets: cognitive outcomes and affective consequences. Studies reported by Block (1971) provide evidence that mastery learning procedures work well in enabling about four-fifths of students to reach a level of achievement which less than one-fifth attain under non-mastery conditions. The time costs for this are typically of the order of 10-20 percent additional time over class-room scheduled time. Of the affective consequences, specific mention should be made of the increased interest and positive attitudes developed towards the subject. The student begins to 'like' the mastery subject and wants more of it. At a deeper level is the student's self-concept. Mastery and its public recognition provide the necessary reinforcement to look upon himself as adequate. Finally, students' perception of alternative learning resources beyond the teacher and text book represents a by-product most important in developing the habit of independent learning of 'life-long education'.

Basic Tasks for Implementing Mastery Learning at School

To implement mastery learning at the school level four tasks are to be performed. They are (i) defining mastery, (ii) planning for mastery, (iii) teaching for mastery and (iv) grading for mastery. Under these four main tasks several sub-tasks are to be accommodated because these serve as important functions.

1st task: The main function of defining 'mastery' by clearly specifying the goals, tests and performance standard at the course (longterm)/unit (short term) level is the communication of the teacher's learning expectations to students.

2nd task: Once mastery has been defined and specified, the next step is to plan for mastery. The essence of planning for mastery is to help the teacher to monitor the student learning on a unit by unit basis. If the evidence gathered from the formative test suggests that the learning of the students is not upto the mark or expectations, then the steps can be re-arranged and reviewed so that desirable degree of learning is attained.

3rd task: In this step students are informed of how they are expected to demonstrate their learning and how their learning will be judged. So they will be told about the grading system. Finally they are told that they will receive extra time and help of the teacher as needed. In this task some corrective or feedback lessons are arranged by the teachers.

4th task: The final major task is to grade the students. Thus some grades like A, B, C, D, etc. are assigned to students based on their performances on the summative tests. Summative tests are administered with the intention to gather cumulative informations regarding the achievement and development of the students.

Research on Mastery Learning

There are many researchers on 'mastery learning models of teaching'. Comprehensive reviews of the research have been conducted by Block and Burns (1976), Bloom (1976), Dolan (1977-78), Burns (1979), Guskey and Gatas (1985) and Cham (1981). Summing all these researches, three major generalisations can be derived.

1. Mastery learning is very effective as the students' learning under mastery-based conditions can retain a major portion more effectively and efficiently, and moreover students develop a sense of self-confidence in their ability to learn.
2. The key to effectiveness of mastery learning lies within the feedback/corrective mechanism. The importance of corrective instruction was established by Block (1970).

3. Mastery learning is differentially effective for different types of students.

So in conclusion we can say 'mastery learning' teaching model represents a major conceptual as well as procedural break-through in the improvement of student learning as well as school teaching.

References

Block, James H. (Ed.) (1971): *Mastery Learning: Theory and Practice*, New York: Holt, Rinehart & Winston.

Bloom, B.S. et al. (1971): *Handbook on Formative and Summative Learning*. New York: McGraw-Hill Book Co.

Carrol, John (1963) : "A Model of School Learning", Teachers College Record, 64.

3.2.10 BTES: Academic Learning Time Model of Classroom Instruction

The Beginning Teacher Evaluation Study (BTES) carried out by the Far West Laboratory for Educational Research and Development in San Francisco, California, U.S.A. in the 1970's has shown a new path in research on Teacher Behaviour and Pupils' Achievement in Elementary School classrooms. The study has developed, tested and pitted into operation, the Academic Learning Time Model of Classroom Instruction. Until the 1960's research on teaching had not received a great deal of attention. By 1975, however, a number of team and individual research efforts had been completed or were underway. Almost all of these studies were cast in the form of process-product analyses, wherein teacher behaviour and classroom characteristics were observed and subsequently related to measures of student achievement and attitudes. Correlation was the frequently used statistics in these studies. The BTES hypothesized that the acquisition of knowledge in the classroom is best conceived as a multi-year process (Fisher and Barliner, 1977). Thus experimental designs that reflect the process-product framework often suffer from problems of ecological validity.

Simple Modification of Process-Product Approach

Researchers on the BTES have proposed a simple modification of the process-product approach to the study of classroom learning. The link between teacher behaviour and student achievement is the ongoing student behaviour in the classroom learning situation. The variable used in the research is the accrued engaged time of a student in a particular content area with materials that are of an easy level of difficulty. This complex variable is called the Academic Learning Time (ALT). This variable ALT, which is measured in real time, has some roots in the work of Carroll (1963), Bloom (1976) and others. The investigations of the relations of ALT to teacher behaviour and to student achievement requires a change to be made in the process-product research paradigm.

This modification may be schematized as in Figure 3.2.6.

The thesis of the BTES is that the marked variability in ALT, between and within classes, is the most potent explanatory variable to account for variability in student achievement, after initial aptitude has been removed as a predictor variable. A corollary to this thesis is that interactive teaching behaviours can only be understood through their effects on ALT. It has been found that teacher behaviour focussed on direct instruction results in longer ALT. Teachers apparently do make a difference, if they act in accordance with some of the common-sense principles, that are used by instructional technologists.

The teacher behaviours, focussing on direct instruction in the classroom, has been identified as five major interlinked teaching activities. These five activities maximise ALT. The link between the activities and with ALT is schematized as in Figure 3.2.6.

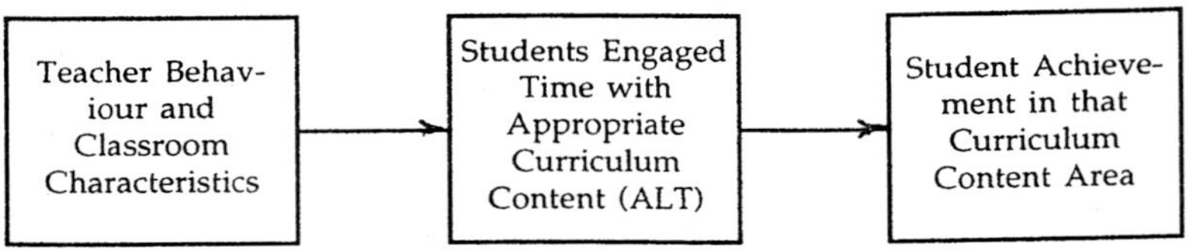

Fig. 3.2.6 Simple Flow of Events that Influence Achievement in a Particular Curriculum Content Area

The teacher behaviours that influence student learning have been conceptualized as serving five interrelated functions. These are diagnosis, prescription, presentation, monitoring, and feedback. These functions are broadly of two categories, planning and interaction; and these functions occur through time in a cyclical fashion as shown in Figure 3.2.7.

As is explicit from Figure 3.2.7, Academic Learning Time Model of Classroom Instruction is developed in the Beginning Teacher Evaluation Study. The major component of the ALT is the classroom allocation of time from both the teacher and student standpoints. Studying the time variable has led the BTES researchers to observe classroom allocation of time of a teacher. Typically, a teacher in the primary grade allocates 50-100 minutes a day to reading and 30-50 minutes to mathematics. From the analysis of teaching protocols taken in the classes of more- and less-effective teachers, it has been found that teachers become constrained by their time allocation, starting and ending lessons by clock rather than on the basis of the cyclical functions

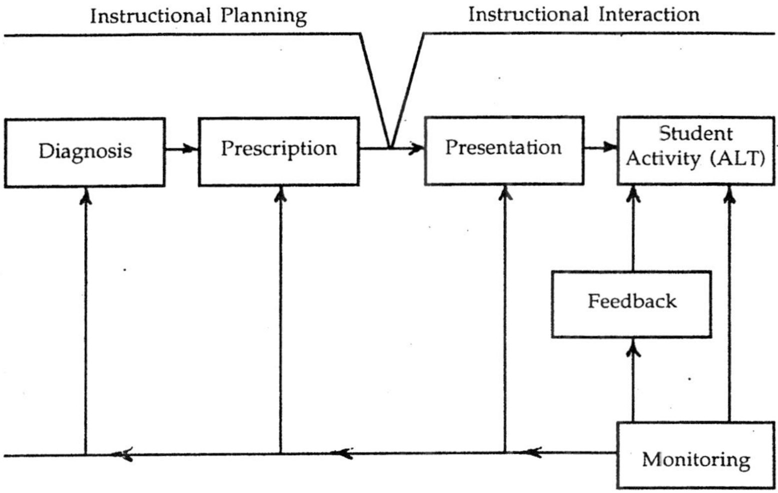

Fig. 3.2.7 Instructional Functions in the Academic Learning Time Model of Classroom Instruction

of the ALT model. Thus when teachers rush students for any reason, skipping one or more functions of the model, they appear to be less effective in helping students achieve in academic areas (Tikunoff, Berliner and Rist, 1975). Immature learners cannot thrive when disjointed lessons occur within a given instructional period. The ALT is synonymous with engagement, attention, and on-task behaviour. Everytime a student is apparently on-task during a teacher's allocated time for a lesson, increase in learning takes place. Even slight increase in ALT would appear to be logically related to increased student acquisition of knowledge. Empirical data from many sources is accumulating to support this proposition (Bloom, 1976).

Conclusion

It may be concluded, on the basis of the BTES research, that at the primary grades, more academic knowledge is acquired by students in classes where (a) the schools and teachers have allocated more time for academic instruction; (b) the time used for lessons is continuous rather than disjointed; (c) teachers are actively oriented rather than bound by clock as a guide for the length of the lesson; and (d) students are actively involved in instructional episode so that differences between the teachers' and students' allocation of time are minimized.

References

Bloom, B.S. (1976): *Human Characteristics and School Learning*. New York: McGraw-Hill.

Fisher, C. W., Berliner, D.C. and others (1978): *Teaching Behaviours Academic Learning Time and Student Achievement:* Final Report of phase - III-B, Beginning Teacher Evaluation Study. Far West Laboratory for Educational Research and Development, San Francisco.

3.2.11 Rosenshine: Direct Instruction (DI) of Structured School Subject

The research on effective teaching on reading and mathematics, conducted since 1970s, has yielded a pattern of instruction that is particularly useful for teaching a body of content or well-defined skills in the classroom situation of a school (Fisher et al., 1978). This pattern of instruction is most effective in any "well-structured" discipline where the objective is to teach performance skills or mastery of a body of knowledge. Specifically, the results of the Fisher et al's research are most applicable to the teaching of mathematical procedures and computations.

The method, called *Direct Instruction (DI)*, is developed on the basis of the observation of more effective teachers teaching in regular classrooms "structured" subjects like mathematics, science and grammar of a language. DI finds its logical support in Information-processing research. The research suggests that it is important for the teacher to provide instructional support for students when teaching new material (Tobias, 1982). Such support occurs when the teacher (i) breaks material into small steps in order to reduce possible confusion, (ii) gives the student active practice in each step in order to move the new learning into long-term memory, and (iii) provides for additional practice and overlearning so that the learners are using the new material on skills effortlessly.

Six Teaching Functions

In summarizing the studies on DI Rosenshine (1986) reports six broad, distinct teaching functions as given in Table 3.2.3.

It has been found that (i) trained and untrained teachers differ in daily review of lessons, (ii) effective teachers spend more time on presenting new materials and guided practice, (iii) students learn quickly and learn better, when particularly process feed back are given. Fisher et al. (1978) have found that students are more engaged during seatwork when the teacher moves around the room and monitors and supervises their work; when teachers give a great deal of explanations during seatwork, students make more errors. Good and Grouws (1979) recommend that teachers review the previous week's work every Monday and the previous month's work every fourth Monday.

These reviews and tests provide additional successful practice for students.

Table 3.2.3 Teaching Functions

1. Daily Review
   — *Review home work*: review relevant, previous learning, review pre-requisite skills and knowledge for the lesson.
2. Presentation
   — State lesson goals and/or provide outline; *teach in steps*; provide concrete example, use clear language, check for student understanding, avoid digressions.
3. Guided Practice
   — Frequent questioning, all of students respond and receive feedback, *high success rate*, continue practice until students are fluent.
4. Corrections and Feedback
   — Give process feedback when answers are correct but hesitant; give clues; reteach for incorrect answers, *reteach when necessary*.
5. Independent Practice
   — Help students during initial steps or overview, *supervise practice until students are automatic*.
6. Weekly/Monthly Review

In sum, DI, in well-structured subjects like mathematics, physics, economics and grammar, is a process in which the teacher initially takes full responsibility for the performance of a task (i.e. lesson), but gradually relinquishes responsibility to the student. This progression can be seen as a continuum that moves from teacher modelling, through guided practice using prompts and cues, to independent and fluent performance by the learner. Research has conclusively shown that DI improves students achievement in school subjects like mathematics, frequently with gains in students' attitude towards the subject, teacher, and themselves.

References

Rosenshine, B.V. (1986): "Synthesis on Research on Explicit Teaching" *Educational Leadership*, 43: 60–69.

Tobias, S. (1982): "When do Instructional Methods Make a Difference?" 11: 4–10.

3.2.12 Shavelson: Decision Making Model of Teaching

Decision making is pervasive in teaching. Descriptive studies have even suggested that the list of instructional decisions made by classroom teachers is infinite. It is related to every aspect of a teachers' professional life, especially in planning, implementing, and evaluating instruction. All teaching is based on decisions made by the teacher after complex cognitive processing of available information.

The heuristic model assumes that teaching is a process by which teachers make rational decisions with the intent of optimizing student outcomes (Shavelson, 1976). This concept is applicable to many goal oriented teaching situations. In this context, teacher is seen as an active agent with many teaching skills and techniques at his or her disposal to help students reach some goal. He must integrate a large amount of information about students from a variety of sources. And this information must somehow be combined with his or her own beliefs and goals, the nature of the instructional task, the constraints of the situation, and so on.

The model in Figure 3.2.8 identifies some important factors which may affect teachers' pedagogical decisions. Teachers have available a large amount of information ("cues") about their students e.g., sex, general ability or achievement, class-participation, self-image, social competence, independence, classroom behaviour and work habits. Teachers categorize students on dimension such as cognitive competence, motivation, behaviour, and social competence. These estimates about students are expected to influence a teacher's plans for instruction, consciously or unconsciously, during instruction.

Individual difference between teachers such as educational beliefs and cognitive styles, influence both their identification and integration of information about students and their pedagogical decisions.

Another flowchart demonstrating a sequence of instructional decisions may help in understanding this kind of analysis of teachers' decision-making (Figure 3.2.10).

The nature of the instructional task—the subject matter, the topic and the type of objective—themselves present a decision-making problem. It may indirectly affect these dimensions by

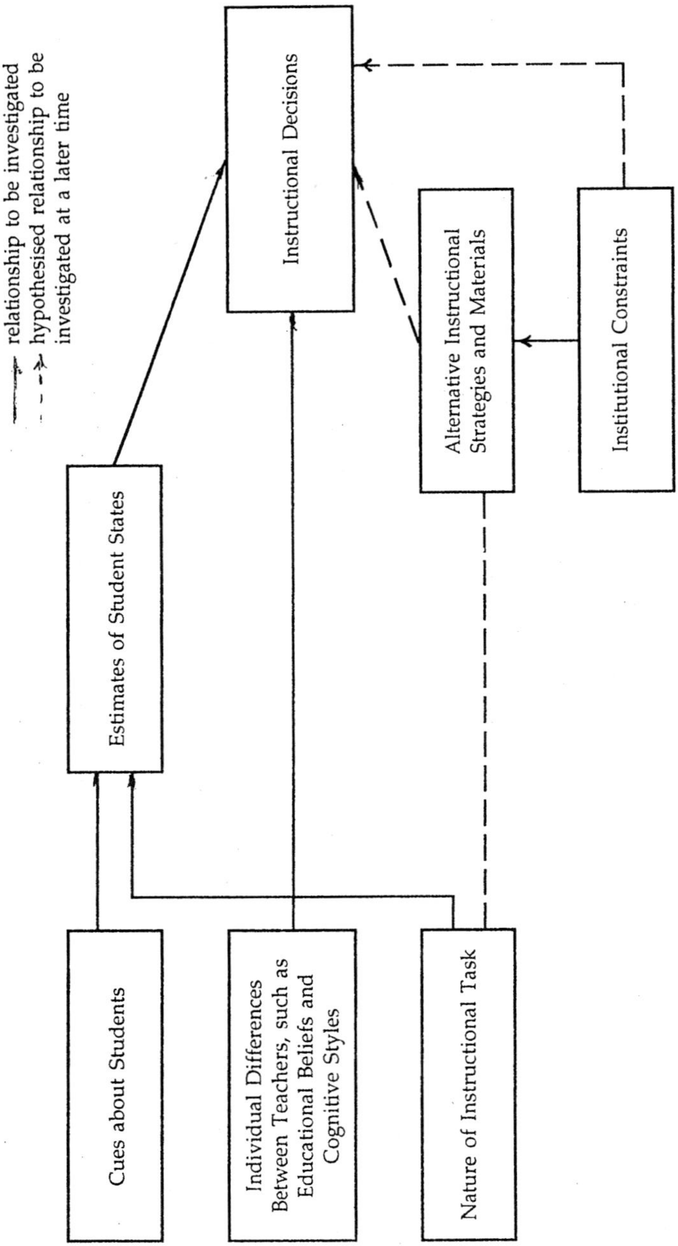

Fig. 3.2.8 Some Factors Contributing to Teachers' Pre-Instructional Decisions

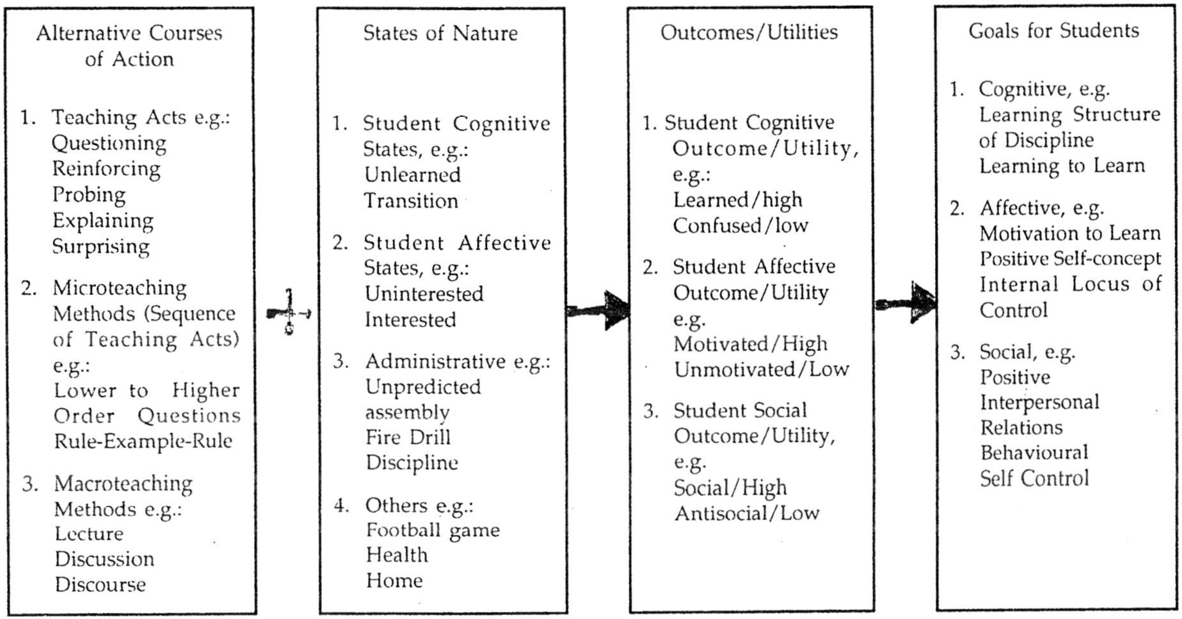

Fig. 3.2.9 Schematic Representation of the Elements in a Decision

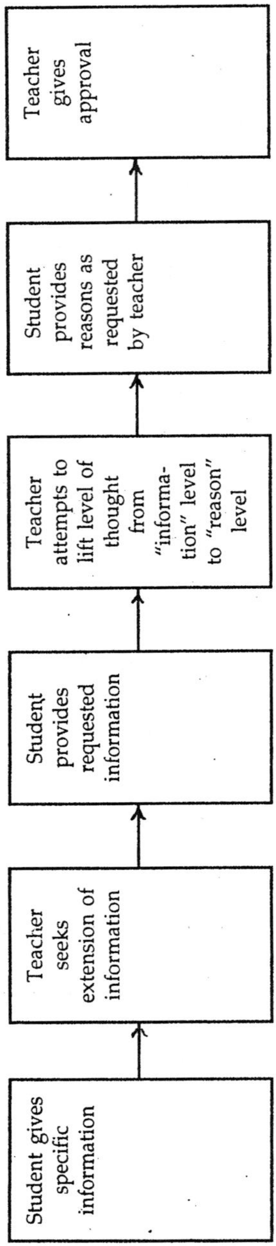

Fig. 3.2.10 Flowchart of Teacher-Child Interaction Illustrating the Sequential Nature of Decision-Making

influencing the cues about the students to which the teacher attends and the estimates about students that are considered relevant to the decision. The curriculum also influences decisions about instruction directly and indirectly by limiting the alternative instructional strategies which the teacher considers when planning a lesson.

Finally, the availability of alternative teaching strategies and materials is also expected to influence decisions directly by limiting the set of possible alternatives from which the teacher may choose. Availability may be influenced by the nature of the instructional task, the teachers' repertoire of strategies, constraints imposed by the institutional environment (e.g., school and classroom), and so on.

The content of teaching as decision-making can be illustrated by five general features of decision. These features deal with teacher decisions intended to optimize student outcomes.

Applications

Decisions made while planning instruction may be the most important ones that teachers make. Unlike decisions during interactive teaching, decisions made in planning can be pondered upon—they have the advantage of time.

Since the teacher is an instructional designer in this pre-tutorial phase of teaching, recommendations for the decisions should help identify decision options available in teaching. Such recommendations generally include from common elements. First, teachers of *students' learning* that are to result from instruction, that is, outcomes, are stated explicitly as observable student behaviour. Second, the students' present capabilities or entry behaviours are identified. Third, an instructional sequence is planned that most likely will move the student from his present capabilities toward the instructional outcomes. The sequence of instructional events is derived from whatever model of learning and motivation the teacher has adopted. Fourth, the outcomes of instruction are evaluated. This information forms the basis for decisions made in designing the cycle of instruction.

In fine, teachers' instructional planning can be characterised as a problem in instructional design that can be described as a decision problem. In the simplest case, the decision problem involves, (a) specifying the outcomes of instruction, (b) specifying instructional design alternatives, (c) specifying students' entry behaviour, (d) estimating the outcome of each combination of an instructional alternative and a state of nature, (e) choosing the optimal course of action and (f) evaluating instruction by observing student behaviour.

The search for basic teaching skills and teaching methods, that lead to specified pupils' outcomes probably will not prove fruitful until facets of the teaching environment—states of nature, student learning states, physical arrangement of the classroom, administrative policies and characteristics of the teacher (values, aptitudes, availability of alternative teaching acts and methods)—are systematically examined. The decision analysis model suggests that these facets should be considered in determining the relation between interactive teaching and student outcomes. Evaluation involves collecting and using information about the correspondence between the actual outcome of a teaching method and the intended outcome of guaging the worth of prior decisions. This information is then extrapolated in making current and future decisions. On the basis of earlier research we best guess that a model of teaching as rational decision making is not unrealistic, with the caveat that teachers, like other persons, are subject to several predictable biases. In this case, teachers need to be trained, if possible, to use evaluative information in a more objective manner to reach decisions that will optimize student outcomes.

However, the major contribution of the decision model is to focus attention on providing teachers with a means for determining teaching acts or methods that are effective for them under certain teaching situations while the findings may vary from teacher to teacher, the cumulative effect would be to improve their teaching.

References

Shavelson, R.J. (1976): Teacher's decision-making, in Gage N.L. (Ed.) *The Psychology of Teaching Methods*, Univ. of Chicago Press, Chicago, Illinois.

Shavelson, R.J. and Stern, P. (1981): Research on Teachers' pedagogical thoughts, Judgments, decisions and behavior, *Review of Educational Research*, 51: 455-498.

3.2.13 Dunkin and Biddle: Model for the Study of Classroom Teaching

The critical observations on the dominant research programmes of early days reflect that the models used for the study of teaching were typically concerned with "Single-interact" ignoring the larger and more complex exchanges that constituted the important features of classroom process.

On the basis of this observation M.J. Dunkin and B.J. Biddle constructed a model for the study of classroom teaching in 1974. In this model there are four variables namely PRESAGE variables, CONTEXT variables, PROCESS variables and PRODUCT variables.

The *presage* variable are nothing but *teacher characteristics* which include teacher's formative experiences from the society, the training experiences he got from universities, practice teaching etc., the teacher properties like his skills, intelligence, personality traits etc.

The *context* variables are chiefly concerned with *student characteristics* such as their formative experiences from home and society, their abilities, knowledge and attitude, their school size, ethnic composition of community, their text books, educational aids and the size of their class etc.

The *process* variables are the *observable actions of teacher* and students at the time of their mutual interaction in the classroom for bringing a change in pupil behaviour.

Finally, the *product* variables refer to the *growth of pupils* that take place as a result of this mutual interaction. This growth is of two types—immediate growth and long term growth. Immediate growth includes learning of subject matter, attitude toward subject, development of different skills etc. and long term growth means the development of adult personality, professional and occupational skills.

The model is shown in Figure 3.2.11.

Reference

Dunkin, M.J. and Biddle, B.J. (1974): *The Study of Teaching*, Holt, Rinehart & Winston, New York.

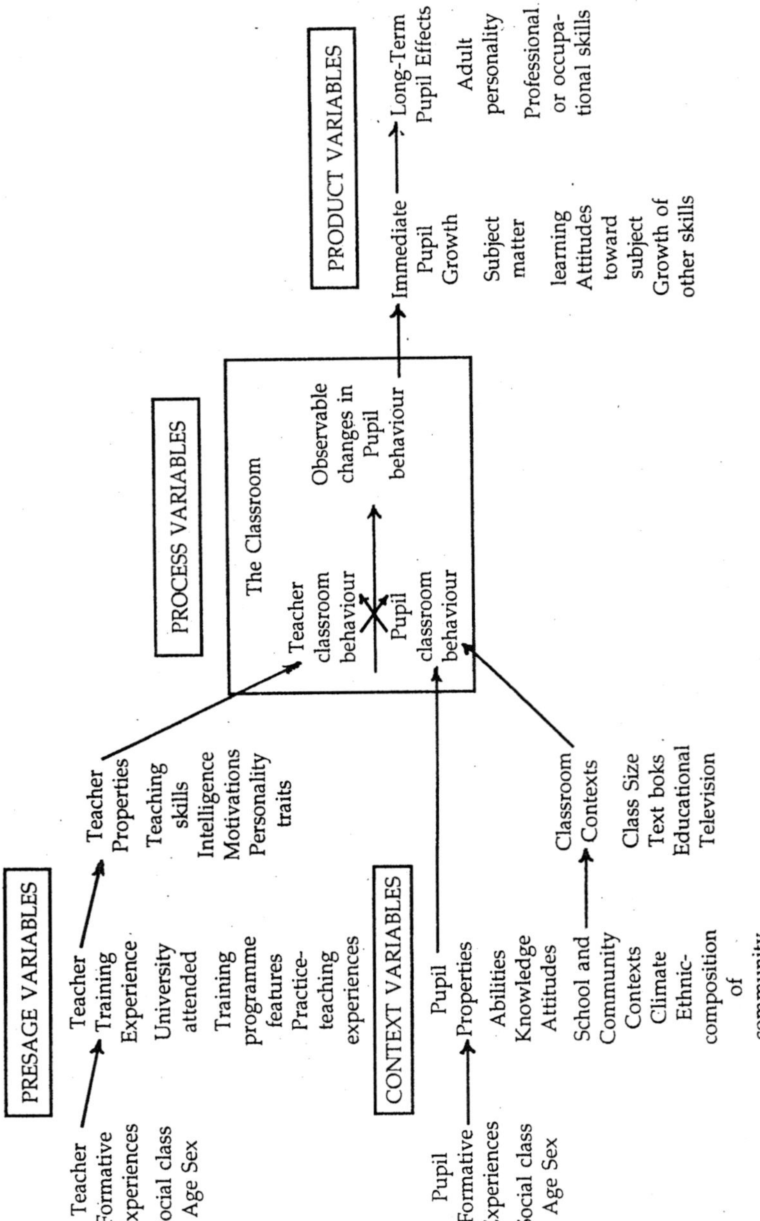
PRESAGE VARIABLES
Teacher Formative Experiences
Social class
Age Sex
Teacher Training Experience
University attended
Training programme features
Practice-teaching experiences
Teacher Properties
Teaching skills
Intelligence
Motivations
Personality traits
CONTEXT VARIABLES
Pupil Formative Experiences
Social class
Age Sex
Pupil Properties
Abilities
Knowledge
Attitudes
School and Community Contexts
Climate
Ethnic-composition of community
Bussing
Classroom Contexts
Class Size
Text boks
Educational Television
PROCESS VARIABLES
The Classroom
Teacher classroom behaviour
Pupil classroom behaviour
Observable changes in Pupil behaviour
PRODUCT VARIABLES
Immediate Pupil Growth
Subject matter learning
Attitudes toward subject
Growth of other skills
Long-Term Pupil Effects
Adult personality
Professional or occupa-tional skills

3.2.14 Lowman: A Two-Dimensional Model of Effective College Teaching

In two-dimensional model of teaching effectiveness, the quality of instruction results from a college teacher's skill at creating both intellectual excitement and positive rapport in students, the kinds of emotions and relationships that motivate them to do their best work. These two kinds of skills are relatively independent, and excellence at either can ensure effective teaching with some students and in certain kinds of classes.

Dimension I: Intellectual Excitement

Skill at creating intellectual excitement has two components; the clarity of an instructor's communications and their positive emotional impact on students. Clarity is related to what one presents, and positive emotional impact results from the way in which material is presented.

Knowledge is far more than the accumulation of isolated facts and figures. It involves a deeper understanding, an ability to "walk around" facts, and, see them from different angles. For a teacher to do an excellent job, he or she must be able to do far more than simply present the details of a subject and students seem to know this. They like to receive an overall perspective and love to compare and contrast different concepts in addition to learning individual facts.

To be able to present material clearly, lecturers must approach and organise their subject matter as if they too know little about it. They must focus on the early observations, essential milestones, key assumptions, and critical insights in a subject and not to be distracted by the qualifications and limitations that most concern themselves as scholars. Being able to do this leads to the ability to explain a complex subject simply.

The ancient Greek and Hebrew teachers were masters of metaphor, making complex points by using simple language and concrete images. Outstanding college teachers are able to explain ideas and the connections between them in ways that make eminently good sense to the uninitiated.

However, understanding material is not the same thing as being intellectually excited about it. For example, being so highly engaged in a presentation as to be free from distracting thoughts and fantasies, surprised when the class-period is over, or compelled to talk about the class to others during the day. To have this kind of impact on students, an instructor must do far more than present material clearly.

This model describes instructors at the big, middle, and lower ranges in this dimension of intellectual excitement. A teacher at the upper end of Dimension I is an unusually skilled individual. To master college teaching to this degree, an instructor must be able to do more than prepare an accurate, well organised synopsis of a content area and deliver the material with the skill of a seasoned speaker.

A teacher at the moderate level is able to organise and deliver the material in an interesting manner, with a moderate level of energy.

A teacher at the lower end is able to organise some material well and present clearly, but much is vague and confusing.

Dimension II: Interpersonal Rapport

In theory, the college classroom is strictly an intellectual and rational arena. In reality, a classroom is a highly emotional interpersonal arena in which a wide range of psychological phenomena occur. For example, students' motivation to work will be reduced, if they feel that they are disliked by their instructor or controlled in heavy-handed or autocratic ways. All students are vulnerable to such disrupting emotions, and some students are especially sensitive to them. Also, like anyone else, students have a potential to react emotionally, when they are being challenged and evaluated in group settings. Even students whose work is superior will become angry if testing and grading practices seem unfair.

Dimension II deals with an instructor's awareness of these interpersonal phenomena and with his or her skill at communicating with students in ways that increase motivation, enjoyment, and independent learning. This is done in essentially two ways. The first is to avoid stimulation of negative emotions, notable excessive anxiety and anger toward the teacher. The second is to promote positive emotions, such as the feeling that the instructor respects the students as individuals and sees them as capable of performing well. These sets of emotions strongly affect students' motivation to complete their assignments and learn material whether their motivation is a desire for approval from the teacher or an attempt to meet their own personal standards.

A teacher at the upper end of Dimension II appears to have strong interest in the students as individuals and acknowledges students' feelings about matters of class assignments.

A teacher at the moderate level is friendly and personable to students but makes no great effort to get to know most of them. He/she is relatively consistent and predictable in behaviour toward students.

A teacher at the lower level of this dimension shows little interest in students as persons. He/she may be inconsistent and unpredictable and occasionally sarcastic or openly disdainful about students.

Combining Dimensions I and II

The Table 3.2.4 above, presents the full model in which Dimensions I and II form nine combinations or cells, each representing a unique style of instruction associated with different probabilities that students will learn to their fullest potential from instructors following that style. The nine styles are numbered in ascending order of overall effectiveness, with Cell one the least effective and Cell nine the most effective.

Table 3.2.4 A Two-Dimensional Model of Effective College Teaching

Dimension I: Intellectual Excitement ↑ / Dimension II: Inter Personal Rapport →	Low (Cold, distant, highly controlling, unpredictable)	Moderate (Relatively warm, approachable and democratic, predictable)	High (Warm, open, predictable, highly student-centred)
High (Extremely clear and exciting)	Cell 6 Intellectual Authority	Cell 8 Master Lecturer	Cell 9 Complete Master
Moderate (Reasonably clear and interesting)	Cell 3 Adequate	Cell 5 Competent	Cell 7 Master Facilitator
Low (Vague and dull)	Cell 1 Inadequate	Cell 2 Marginal	Cell 4 Socratic

Instructors in Cells 1, 2 and 3 are less than fully competent. The "adequate" will be minimally successful in lecture classes and with relatively compliant students, but need increased interpersonal skill to expand the range of students and situations in which he will be effective. Similarly, the "Marginal" need to improve their ability to present material. Teachers in Cells 4 and 6 represent the most unusual combinations of skills. The "Socratic" excels at promoting independent work and will be ideal for students and subjects well suited to seminars. Their approach will be inadequate in larger classes requiring lecturing, however. Conversely, the "Intellectual Authority" will be able to create intellectual excitement and promote achievement in students, who are confident in their own abilities and comfortable with such instructor's distant manner, but younger or less able students are likely to experience anxiety under such instruction. An "Intellectual Authority" is more likely to be respected than loved by most students.

All instructors in Cells 7, 8 and 9 are outstanding individuals, who have unquestionably attained excellence at college teaching. Students are likely to describe a "Masterful Lecturer" as one who captivates them by sheer intellectual force and motivates them to learn material because it seems a terribly important and exciting thing to do.

In contrast, students of 'Masterful Facilitator' feel close to their instructors. Such instructors are likely to be able to stimulate independent work of high quality. They are sought out by students after class and are particularly effective in smaller, more advanced classes characterized by considerable discussion. They are also likely to become important in their students' personal lives; students may come to them for advice or attempt to model their lives or careers after them. Both "Masterful Lecturer" and "Masterful Facilitator" have their fortes, but each is capable of providing competent instruction in all situations.

The rare "Complete Master" of Cell 9 is able to perform superbly in both lecture-hall and seminar-room and to modify his approach so as to motivate all students, from the brilliant to the mediocre.

Most students will do well under Cells 7, 8 or 9 instructor, and are likely to rate all these masterful types highly, but they may prefer one type or the other.

Outstanding instructors, then are those who excel at one or both of these two dimensions of teaching effectiveness. Every competent teacher must have at least moderate skill in each dimension, but there is considerable room for variation. According to Lowman (1984), some students will learn more under one style of instructor than another, but that all students will learn more and prefer college teachers in the masterful cells (i.e. Cells 7, 8 and 9). He also assumes that instructors' skills in Dimensions I and II are distributed normally; that is, that most teachers are competent, falling at the midrange of each dimension, and relatively few are above or below the norm.

Reference

Lowman, J. (1984): *Mastering the Techniques of Teaching*, Prentice-Hall of India, New Delhi.

3.2.15 MITRA*: THE PSYCHOLOGICAL MODEL OF TEACHING—THEORY OF INSTRUCTION

Mitra conceives teaching as a formalised instructional situation where two persons are bound by a contractual relationship in order to carry out a series of acts with a specific aim in view. Mitra has himself acknowledged that he has been deeply impressed by Gage's Handbook of Research on Teaching (1963). Mitra has also accommodated in his theory some elements from Bruner's 'Theory of Instruction'. In his theory of instruction, Mitra has incorporated two psychological variables, namely, the 'contractual' aspect of teaching situation and the 'cognitive map' which guides the instructional process. We shall briefly explain what these two psychological variables mean in Mitra's Model of Teaching.

Contractual Relationship

Mitra believes that teacher and students are bound by a contractual relationship in a classroom situation. The contractual relationship in the teaching situation is embedded in a socio-cultural matrix. The teacher has to operate often within a network of institutional and informal relationships. He has overlapping memberships of various groups both formal and informal. These relationships can be conceptualised as roles given, acquired and received by the teacher. It is, however, important to understand the relationship network centering around the teacher, how these crystallize into roles, generate conflicts and thereby change a straight-forward contract. Values in the society and culture have an important bearing on this. The value attached to a contractual relationship in a culture is related to other values. Thus in a society teaching is accorded a high value, very often altruistic value, as a result of which the values attached to a contract are de-emphasised, and it may generate a conflict not only between the teacher and the pupils, but in the inter-personal situation of teaching itself. In the process, the act of teaching takes a course which is not strictly determined by the contract and the teaching task. Teaching encompasses a lot of things which can be clearly understood in the framework of the theory of conflict resolution.

* Shib K. Mitra was an eminent Professor of Educational Psychology in India; he retired as Director, the N.C.E.R.T. New Delhi.

The contract in a teaching situation implies that the teacher will give instruction and lesson, explain and illustrate, elucidate and elaborate, evaluate, make critical appraisal and so on. The pupil, in turn, will think, observe, analyse, reason, appreciate, evaluate and so on. Basically the teacher gives an idea or shows certain ways of doing things. If these do not satisfy the needs of the pupils, the teacher varies his behaviour, until he thinks that pupils' requirements have been met. The situation is dynamic in the sense that the demand and supply interact and mutually influence thereby bringing changes in both, until the process finds its own equilibrium, where the student feels that his requirement has been fulfilled or it ends up in a disequilibrium or discord, where the student feels his needs have not been met.

Cognitive Map

Another important factor, having bearing on the instructional process, is the cognitive map of the teacher. The teacher has to consider the formulation of the teaching task in a given situation, by making an assessment of the stage of development of the learner with respect to the learning outcome finally to be achieved. The teacher has to make decisions about the complexity of the materials like subject-matter presented, the previous knowledge of the students, the mode of delivery of the material. In doing all these, a teacher should have a 'cognitive map' in his mind in which there is a definite goal and where a path to the goal is chalked out in terms of the subject matter knowledge under consideration. Though there is scope for individual organisation of the cognitive map, it is limited usually by the logic of the subject or the structure of the discipline. The cognitive map is widely shared by teachers and has more or less clear-cut, area-wise, step-wise divisions, which the learner has to pass to reach mastery. The teacher's task is to make an assessment of the position of the pupil on this map where he is at the moment, how far he has to go, in which direction, etc. In order to know this he may either elicit responses in a pre-arranged or spontaneous manner, or depend on his recollection of responses already made by the pupil earlier. What is important to note is that the teacher must have a differentiated cognitive map of the behaviour domain for which he is responsible, and he must observe the pupil behaviours relevant to the behaviour domain and make a judgement about his position on the map.

Mitra's Theory of Instruction

Mitra (1971) divides theories of teaching into two broad categories.

1. In the first category teacher behaviour is treated as a dependent variable.
2. The second category considers teacher behaviour as an independent variable.

Mitra lists under first category such theories as 'Role Theory' 'Personality Theory' and 'Learning Theory'. We say that, if there are certain kinds of roles which the teacher has learned, then the teacher will behave in a certain way and this is the 'Role Theory'; or if the teacher has certain types of personality characteristics, then he will behave in a particular fashion, this is the 'Personality Theory', or if the teacher has been trained to behave in a certain way, he produces that kind of behaviour and this is the 'Learning Theory.' It is obvious that in all these cases, the teacher behaviour is a dependent variable in the sense that it can not be manipulated. What we want to find out is the kind of variation in this behaviour, which is produced by variations elsewhere like his own personality, the class room, the society and the culture.

The second type of theory tries to explain how interpersonal influence results in learning with the teacher behaviour as an independent variable. Mitra states that a theory of teaching must aim at explaining how this interpersonal influence really induces behaviour modification in the learner. This may be explained with the help of conditioning theory, identification theory and cognitive re-structuring theory, wherein each theory has led to a research movement in teaching.

Broadly, seven classes of variables are treated as independent variables which have bearing on teacher behaviour (Figure 3.2.12). Of these seven variables, three, namely, grade level, subject matter and social background of teacher and students, are either controlled in any actual research, or kept in the background.

Teacher behaviour is represented as a dependent variable. It should be read from left to right. Also indicated therein are some of more explicitly stated relationships between the independent variables by means of arrows. The two variables namely media of teaching and instruments of teaching are placed together as a suggestion by way of simplification of the paradigm.

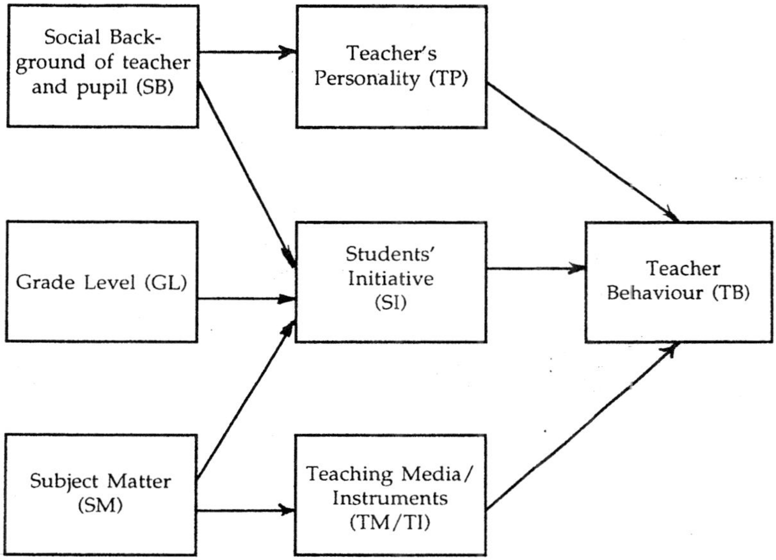

Fig. 3.2.12 Teacher Behaviour as Dependent Variable

Mitra in 1971 has given a paradigm depicted in Figure 3.2.13 which shows teacher behaviour as an independent variable. Teacher produces a classroom atmosphere of learning. It is something more than social interaction which is an antecedent condition of teaching. The teacher produces a climate, also delivers stimuli and arranges the condition of reinforcement and facilitates the production of responses.

Now both the classroom atmosphere and arrangements for learning converge on the learning of pupils and this in turn, produces two measurable outcomes, namely pupil growth over a period of time and the achievement of pupils at any point of time.

Finally, Mitra combines Figures 3.2.12 and 3.2.13 into a 'Gestalt', which we may call an 'Educational Planning Model'.

The composite paradigm is depicted in Figure 3.2.14.

It combines the modes of teacher behaviour both as dependent and independent variables. This composite figure is more than juxtaposition of Figure 3.2.12 and Figure 3.2.13. It incorporates two psychological variables from Mitra's theory, namely

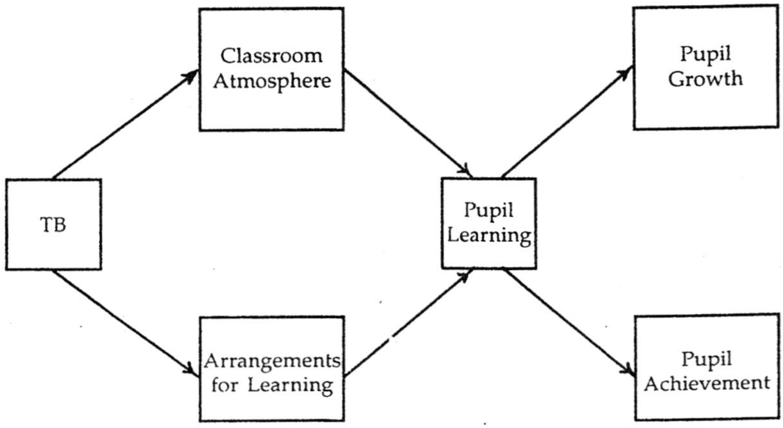

Fig. 3.2.13 Teacher Behaviour (TB) as Independent Variable

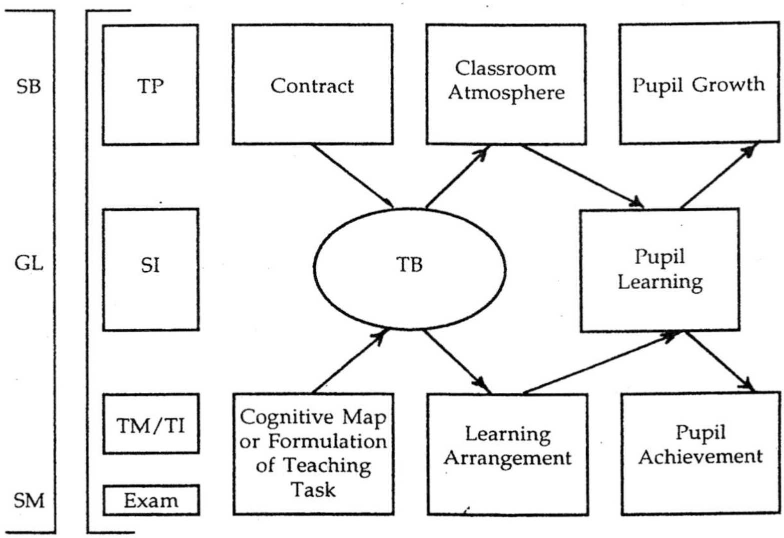

Fig. 3.2.14 Composite Model of Teacher Behaviour (TB)

the 'contractual aspect of the teaching situation' and the 'cognitive map' which guide the instructional process. These two are on the side of antecedent conditions of teaching, and according to Mitra the two are the proximate, or immediately proceeding, antecedents of teaching.

Reference

Mitra, S.K. (1970): "Psychology of Teaching: Rudiments of a Theory", Presidential Address, Psychology and Educational Science Section, 57 *Indian Science Congress*, III, Kharagpur, India.

3.2.16 Arthur and Bolster: Ethnograpic Model of Teaching

The complex process of teaching is conceived and defined differently giving emphasis mostly to one of these aspects either as an interpersonal influence in the social context wherein the person changes the ways in which other persons can or will behave or as a set of well-defined and sequenced activities predetermined so as to bring about learning in pupils (emphasis on the outcome). Whatever may be the emphasis either to process or product, both the approaches agree that teaching involves a process of interaction between the teacher and a class of pupils. This section elaborates on this concept of teaching, pointing out the merits and demerits of the methodology employed so far by many researchers to understand the process, suggests an alternative model for research giving more emphasis to ethnographic approach.

Teaching—As it is

Teaching may be conceived as an interactive problem-solving process which involves a series of teaching situations wherein the teacher has to take decisions about how he should behave such that it appears to be reflexive rather than reflective. The teacher, apart from the intentions of bringing about learning outcomes in pupils, has a set of beliefs (which also includes perceptions and role expectations of himself and of pupils), values and norms of behaviour which determine his behaviour. This behaviour would in turn be interpreted differently by different pupils depending on *their* beliefs, values and perceived norms for behaviour and all these would determine the pupil's behaviour. This, in turn, leads to producing certain cues by them which again are differently interpreted by the teacher, depending on *his* values, beliefs and norms, leading to his reciprocatory behaviour. The teacher develops, modifies or retains, more or less the same, his systems of beliefs, values and norms during his continual participation in the situational decision-making process. Those instructional behaviours that are consistent with his predictions or 'workables' get strengthened. When he acts, he observes responses to his actions and interprets the meanings of those responses. Since teacher takes decisions depending on the situational variables, it may appear that the process involves mere common sense; but it is a highly complex intellectual task. Thus a teacher needs to be aware of all the situational variables and their likely effects with or without their manipulation and be able to either manipulate them or adopt his behaviour so as to bring out desired outcomes in pupils. This awareness of the teacher is idiographic and particularistic in character (Arthur and Bolster, 1983). That is, the teacher attempts to understand the complexity of the particular context with sufficient accuracy more by intuitive analysis rather than from a comparison of a set of similar situations. His behaviour is pragmatic in character which works on the principle 'that which works'. What he decides to do at any moment is likely to depend on what has just occurred at that particular circumstance. Once he develops a set of beliefs, values and norms, he does not feel the need to have additional experiences to solve situational problems; he develops resistance to change. Thus he develops certain generalised patterns of behaviour.

A Case for Ethnographic Approach

Teaching as a process of social interaction is based on the following assumptions:

(a) Teacher and pupil behaviour is reflexive;
(b) They have shared meanings of the elements in the classroom situation (social, which are derived during the process of classroom interaction and which shape their behaviour). The meanings and hence the behaviours vary from classroom to classroom. Hence there is a need to develop explanations for how a classroom works instead of deriving universal generalizations to explain teacher-pupil behaviour in the classroom. The methodology for such an enquiry should be ethnographic since experimental method does not help in studying the phenomena in a natural setting.

The Approach—Elaborated

Lalitha (1984) says that ethnographic methodology when employed to the study of teaching process would involve writing critical descriptions of what goes on in specific classrooms in terms of what participants do and say in the setting. Each of such descriptions includes:

i) Details of belief, values, and norms of the teacher which are partly included in his lesson plan;
ii) Description of beliefs, values and norms of the group identifying the individual variations if any.
These are identified through interview technique. The descriptions related to these are both descriptive and interpretive.
iii) Description of the physical properties of the setting of the classroom.
iv) Systemic and detailed observations about the behaviour.

Descriptions related to (iii) and (iv) are derived mainly from participant-observation technique. Other measurement techniques although to a limited extent may also be used to describe all the situational variables. But care must be taken such that the latter would be more descriptive rather than interpretive.

Based on the above observations explanatory propositions are derived for each of the specific situations in the classroom. Such explanations are treated as hypotheses which define as specifically as possible the relationships between classroom events in the light of contextual properties associated with them.

Such hypothetical observations are tested in future observations. These patterns of relationships are refined in the light of new data.

Thus, the initial descriptions developed above are validated referentially and situationally. The generalizations which are explanatory must be consistent with repeated patterns of events recorded in the observational data and must be consistent with the meanings teachers and students draw from and impose upon the classroom situation (Arthur and Bolster, 1983). There must also be consistency in the interpretations/explanations made between observers.

The following are the implications of the application of the above methodology to understand teaching:

a) There is a need to evolve a methodology for comprehensive observation of the on-going events in the classroom. This should cover observation of teacher-student behaviours in all the three domains—cognitive, affective and psycho-motor. The detailed linguistic analysis of various concepts and terminologies used in observation has to be presented. As far as possible, all the high inference observations have to be explained in terms of low inference behaviours. More emphasis should be given to establishing construct validity for such observations.

b) From the analysis of descriptions of several teaching situations, hypothetico-deductive theories of instruction can be evolved which would have their limitations to the extent the unique features of each situations affect them.

c) Teacher training involves presenting these varied situations in teaching to the trainees who learn to take decisions which are reflective and deliberate in the beginning and reflexive at a later stage. The assessment of teacher-trainees is made in terms of their responses to a series of classroom situations.

Conclusion

The scientific method is not adequate and sometimes relevant to the study of a social phenomena namely, 'teaching'. Ethnographic method, although difficult to employ in a systematic way, is more suited for understanding what goes on in the classroom.

References

Arthur and Bolster, J. (1983): Toward a More Effective Model of Research on Teaching, *Harvard Educational Review*, 53(3).

Lalitha, M.S. (1984): An Alternative Model for Research on Teaching, paper presented in National Seminar on 'Research on Instruction,' March 22-24, CAS in Education, M.S. University of Baroda, Baroda.

Thapan, M. (1991): *Life at School: An Ethnographic Study*, Oxford University Press, New Delhi.

3.2.17 Landa: Teaching Algorithm

Algorithm is a computational process, leading from various initial data to the desired result. It is defined as "an instruction or an action guide for any operation". More precisely, it is "an exact recipe for the sequence of operations to be carried out within a system, which will lead to the solution of all problems of a given type".

Professor Landa, is the main exponent of 'teaching algorithm'. Although the word 'algorithm' is borrowed from mathematics, but in teaching it is not restricted only to mathematical recipe. In connection with teaching, the concept is extended to cover any rule of thumb procedure for achieving desired outcome. It consists of a flow chart or its list structure equivalent. It provides the user with an algorithm, for handling a variety of different conditions in the right way. A person working through an algorithm is like a computer working through a programme. The process is automatic in both the cases. A successful outcome results, if there be no ambiguity of the instruction.

An algorithmic chart contains a set of test questions. The questions are arranged in an order, which is both convenient and natural. It also contains a corresponding set of conclusions to which particular sequences of answers point.

When an algorithm has been constructed the next phase is to show the operator how to use it. Here the constructors are faced with minimal requirements of showing operators how to use it.

It is needless to say that algorithms should be clear, self-explanatory and intelligible to the recipient who should need no special training. If the task is complex, it requires a long algorithm. The operators might require to memorise and to understand and to learn it. The objective of all algorithmic approach is to get people to use algorithms efficiently.

One of the interesting properties of algorithm is that they can be applied ritualistically without comprehension. This property may be applied to low-level staff to complete high-level task. But the aim of teaching should be the understanding of algorithm that the worker is using. So the trainee should be able to justify the algorithm in relevant ways. It is worth remembering that algorithms can be worded in a way which guarantees some minimum level of understanding.

According to many for many kinds of free prose, no algorithm construction is possible. In case of certain deduction disciplines like mathematics, physics, chemistry etc., the correctness of an algorithm can sometimes be demonstrated from theoretical considerations. But in case of less rigorous disciplines like medicine, law and official regulations there may only be a few guiding principles, based on current knowledge of the subject.

The Russian algorithms are used in the programming of auto-instructional devices. The novelty of the Soviet programme's proposal is to use algorithms, a method to programme certain learning materials. They suggest that the student be given a reference card containing the appropriate algorithm and told to solve the problem in hand. After he has done several problems of the same nature, the reference card is withdrawn. The expectation is that the procedure should now become automatic.

In an experimental study of the effectiveness of algorithms, student had to clarify certain types of sentences. The experimental group had been taught by algorithm and the 7 control groups by conventional methods. They were given sheets with 40 sentences and had to provide the punctuation. Table 3.2.5 refers to average number of mistakes.

Table 3.2.5

Experimental group (Algorithm users)	Control group (Conventional learners)						
	1	2	3	4	5	6	7
3.1	15.5	15.6	19.1	19.5	20.6	25.0	28.3

In conclusion it may be said that students who have been trained in algorithmization have not only learnt to solve concrete problems but have acquired generally useful methods of thinking.

Reference

Edwards, K.F. (1967): "Programmed Learning in the Soviet Block Countries." In Unwin, Derick and Leedham, J. (Eds.) *Aspects of Educational Technology.* Methuen, London.

3.2.18 Allen & Ryan: Micro-teaching

Definition of Micro-Teaching

Micro-teaching is a technique of training teachers to acquire, practice and develop specific teaching skills. Micro-teaching is a system of controlled practice that makes it possible to concentrate on specific teaching skills and to practice teaching under controlled, scaled down conditions.

According to Allen and Ryan (1969) there are five essential propositions at the core of the concept of Micro-teaching.

First: Micro-teaching is real teaching.

Second: It simplifies the class-room teaching in terms of class size, time, content, etc.

Third: It focusses on training for the accomplishment of specific tasks.

Fourth: Micro-teaching allows for the increased control of practice. In the practice setting of micro-teaching, the rituals of time, students, methods of feedback and supervision, and many other factors can be manipulated, consequently, a high degree of control can be built into the teaching programme.

Fifth: Micro-teaching greatly expands the normal knowledge of results or feedback dimension in teaching. Immediately after teaching a micro-lesson, the trainee gets feedback about his performance and several sources of feedback may be used.

Micro-teaching reduces the complexities of the teaching situation in terms of (i) number of students to be taught, (ii) duration of the lesson, (iii) subject matter to be taught to enable the trainee to concentrate on a particular component of the task of teaching, before he attempts to perform effectively the complicated task of teaching at macro-level in class-room situation.

Teaching Skills

Teaching skill is an important characteristics of micro-teaching. Allen and Ryan (1969) have suggested the following fourteen skills:

i) Stimulus variation,
ii) Set induction,
iii) Closure,
iv) Silence and non-verbal cues,
v) Reinforcement of student participation,
vi) Fluency in asking questions,
vii) Probing questions,
viii) Higher order questions,
ix) Divergent questions,
x) Recognising attending behaviour,
xi) Illustrations and use of examples,
xii) Lecturing,
xiii) Planned repetition,
xiv) Completeness of communication.

The Australian Advisory Committee on Research and Development in Education have analysed teaching into 140 skills.

Teaching can be analysed in terms of teaching skills and teaching behaviours at three levels viz. component teaching skills, component teaching behaviours and atomistic teaching behaviour. This is shown in Figure 3.2.15.

T = Teaching
S = Teaching skills
C = Component teaching behaviours that a teaching skill is made of
tb = Atomistic teaching behaviour.

Procedure

(a) Orientation Phase

Micro-teaching is a laboratory technique in which the complexities of normal classroom teaching are simplified (Figure 3.2.16). The trainee teaches a class of about *five* students. The lesson is reduced to *five to ten* minutes. The micro-lesson is used for the practice of one particular teaching skill—lecturing, or questioning or leading a discussion or using instructional aids or closing a lesson. The lesson is recorded on video-tape and the trainee hears and observes himself immediately after the lesson.

In the micro-teaching the analyses and suggestions of a supervisor, who attended the lesson and observed the video-tape,

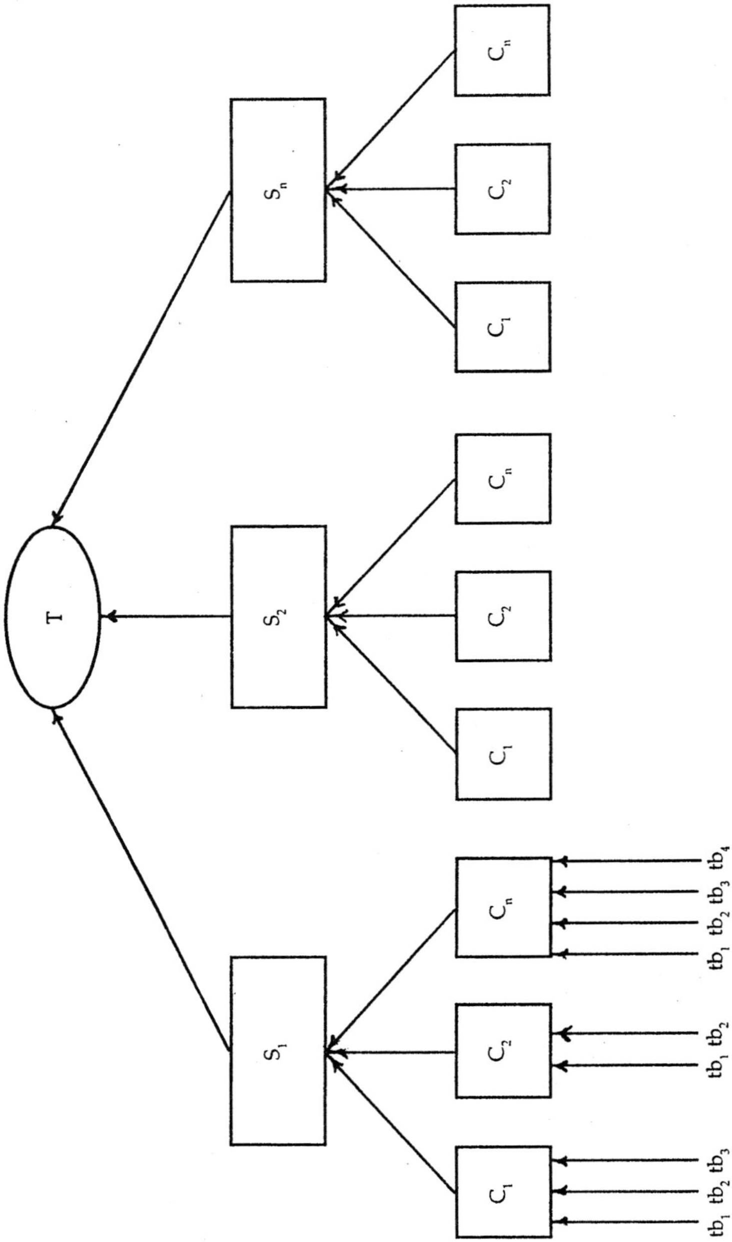

Fig. 3.2.15 Teacher Behaviour Based Concept of Teaching

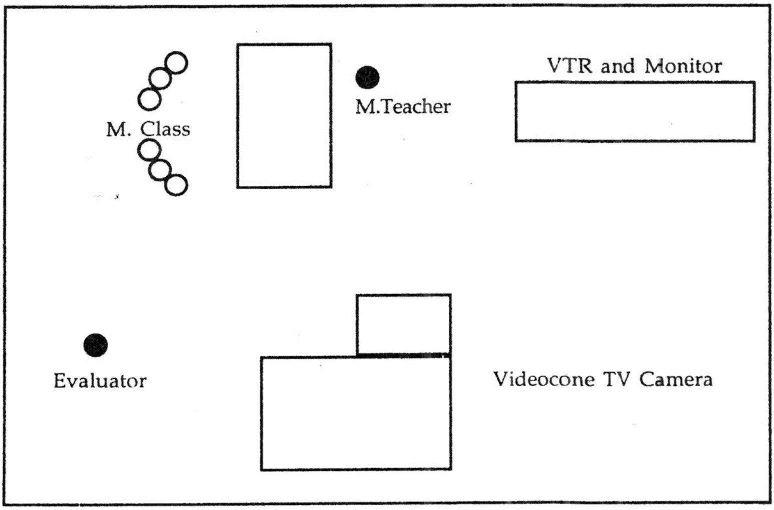

Fig. 3.2.16 Typical Equipment Arrangement in a Micro-Teaching Laboratory

assist the trainee in restricting the lesson. Video-tape recording provides the trainee and the supervisor a common, objective frame of reference of critiquing a trainee's performance immediately after it is completed. The advantage of such attributes are pointed out by extensive psychological research on effect of feedback, including knowledge of result, trial and error learning and reinforcement.

(b) Practice Phase

Current literature on Micro-teaching tends to describe the micro-teaching technique in terms of a "teach-critique-reteach" cycle. The trainee teaches a lesson, views a recording, makes a critique with the help of a supervisor, rethinks, restructures the lesson. This step completes the first session. The second begins with the trainee reteaching the lesson, then again reviews, re-critiques, rethinks and restructures the lesson. Finally he teaches the lesson for the third time when the lesson is appropriately delivered. Figure 3.2.17 shows the complete micro-session to exercise a teaching skill.

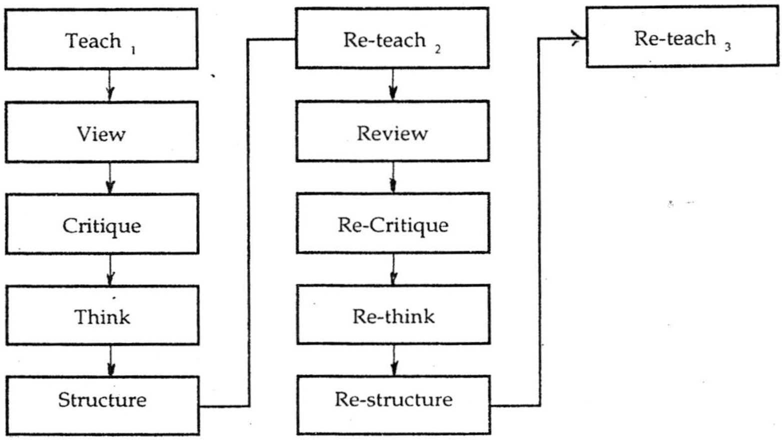

Fig. 3.2.17 Complete Micro-Session Steps

(c) Advantages of Micro-teaching

The main advantages of Micro-teaching are methodological and logistical.

Students are faced with less complicated stimuli than they encounter on conventional school practice.

Supervisors can focus their attention on a particular strength or weakness.

A wide variety of teaching environments and purposes can be conveniently generated.

The intensity of micro-practice can be changed systematically by increasing the length of the lesson or the number of students.

The students and staff are not involved in tedious travelling to and from schools, a much closer control is kept over what each student has actually done and what he needs to do.

Assessment is more reliable and can be jointly done in different cases.

Micro-teaching is also probably cheaper than school practice, but it is very difficult to make a useful comparison.

(d) Limitations of Micro-teaching

Micro-teaching is skill-oriented rather than content-oriented. But the content, which forms the most important component of the teaching-learning process, is not paid adequate attention. In micro-teaching emphasis is laid on specific skills, leaving integration of skills to natural consequences. The scope of micro-teaching is narrow. Hence the entire process of teaching is not covered by micro-teaching. The process of teaching is not the sum total of independent and isolated teaching skills.

In India, micro-teaching is beginning to be a rather widely known, if somewhat less widely applied technique in teacher education and educational research.

References

Allen, D.W. and Ryan, K. (1969): *Microteaching* Addison-Wesley, Reading, Mass.

Bhattacharya, S.P. (1975): Micro teaching in the Training of Polytechnic Teachers, M.S. Univ. Baroda (Unpublished Ph.D. thesis).

3.2.19 Lundgren: Frame Factor Theory of Teaching

Lundgren's (1972) thesis is that if we are to understand, study, analyze or change the teaching process, it is necessary to see it as a process occurring within limits; that it is to some extent governed or steered by the frames the curriculum establishes in its goals and content, the organizational frame established by a group of pupils in the class—we call them the 'steering group' and the 'time-frame' time available for instruction.

Lundgren's theoretical model is simple and we show its three components in a paradigm (Figure 3.2.18).

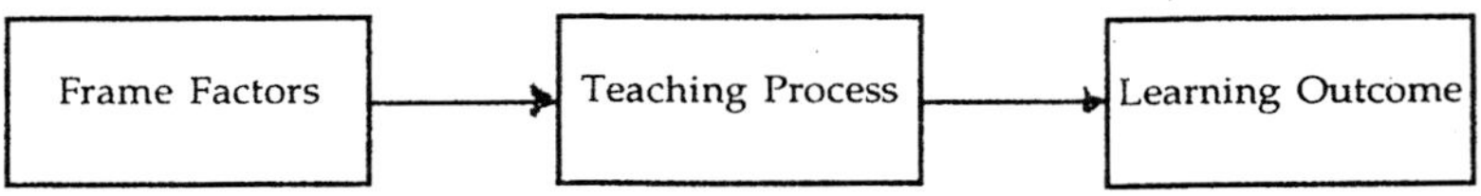

Fig. 3.2.18 A Paradigm of the General Approach and the Outlines of a Model of Teaching

How does this model differ from other models or theories on these relations?

The first component is the concept of frame factors. These are three:

a) Factors given in the curriculum—goals and content;
b) Time available for instruction; and
c) The composition of the class according to the time different pupils need to reach a certain goal.

Since, the teaching process is a *steered* process of communication between different individuals; it seems influencing the person who is regarded as steering the process—i.e. the teacher. Curriculum theory has tried to apply various learning theories or theories of cognitive processes in an educational context.

Another approach to the relationship between curriculum and teaching process has been to concentrate on the philosophy underlying the choice of goals and content.

The model that Lundgren presents is not an alternative to these two approaches, but must be regarded as a third approach for describing the relationship between curriculum and teaching process.

"We see the composition of the class and the time available as the main frames for the teaching process. Together with other limiting factors, such as the goals, the content and the way the content is organized; they limit the ways of forming the teaching process. If the interrelations between these factors can be determined in connection with the actual teaching, the theories based on learning or cognitive process can be used in a pedagogical model."

Dahllof's study (1971) gave the outlines of a theory explaining the relations between the steering group and the time spent on different curriculum units in traditional class instruction. Dahllof located this group as the pupils between percentile 10-25 in respect to intellectual ability. According to his view that, the teaching process, within the existing frames, is assumed to be optimal in relation to the intended outcomes. Total time must here be seen as a special 'frame factor'. We use the term 'time-frame'. We have two groups of variables, frame variables and process variables. Within the time frame given, the process variables are interrelated to shape the most optimal outcome within the other given frames. This is the starting point. The actual teaching may, for different reasons, be carried out in such a way that it is not always optimal. The relations between frame factors and teaching process are one sided. It is assumed that the frame factors to some extent determine the interrelations of the process variables. This is a question of limits—the frame factors limit the possible interrelations between process variables.

But the frame factors do not alone determine the form of the teaching process. The frames limit the variation into the process. If we see the frame factors as predictors of the pace and form of the teaching process, it would be reasonable to assume that these factors explain about 10-25 % of the variance in various measures of the teaching process.

So, how to comprehend the various frame factors? In the earlier studies the frame factors have been defined as 'organisational measures' (Figure 3.2.19).

From the teacher's point of view, curriculum will be included as a frame factor, but if we define frame factors as factors which limit the variation of the teaching process, the curriculum will, from the teacher's point of view, function as a frame factor. In relation to our general and specific models, we have to distinguish between 'curriculum frames' and 'organizational frames'.

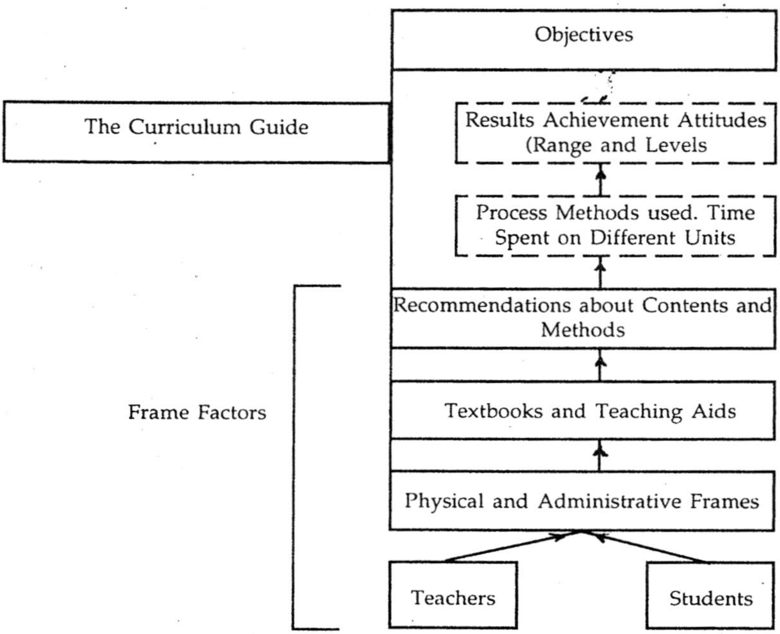

Fig. 3.2.19 Paradigm of the Relations between Frame Factors, Curriculum, Teaching Process and Learning Outcome. (From Dahllof, Lundgren & Sido 1971, p. 102)

We shall use three types of frame factors in our specific model, and it builds on the assumption that the teaching is traditional classroom instruction. By traditional classroom instruction we mean "front of the class teaching" where the teacher verbally or with the help of various simple teaching aids and materials teaches the whole class at the same time.

The first factor is the objectives of the teaching. This factor is a variable in so far as it can vary in exactitude. The second factor is the sequence of content units, within which the various educational goals can be reached. The third factor is the groups into which the pupils fall with regard to the time needed by different pupils to master the units. We may speak of these three factors as variables.

These decisions are dependent on the curriculum and the organisational measures (ability, grouping and size of class etc.) and on the teacher's perception of them, as well as on his conception of his duty as a teacher toward the class he is teaching.

The steering group, as defined in earlier studies, arises when the total time is insufficient to satisfy the three factors. In this way, the steering group becomes the functional expression for the interrelations between these three factors within the time frame, and will in its turn play a role in determining the forming of the teaching process. We can clarify this in a simple way in a paradigm (Figure 3.2.20). As teaching process variables, we shall, throughout, work with three concepts: content, activity and persons involved. The most difficult distinction to make is between the concepts—curriculum and instruction. As we earlier pointed out the term curriculum stands for what is to be taught and how. When we speak of goals and sequence of content units as frame factors, we may see these as expressions of the type of curriculum we shall work with here. If we see the teaching process as to some extent formed by frame factors, we may say that these limit the process, but that these limitations will also depend on the weight that is given to content and activity. This is a highly simplified presentation of a very dynamic relation existing between different concepts. Nevertheless, we shall try to express

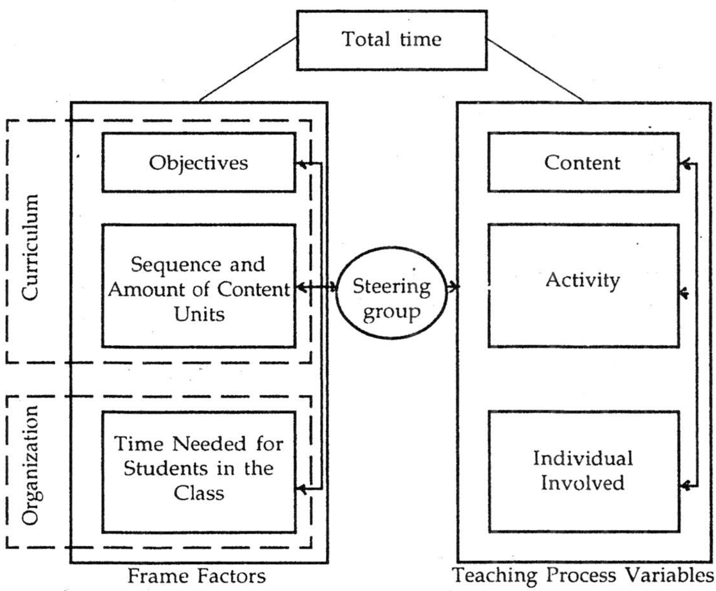

Fig. 3.2.20 Paradigm of the Relations Postulated as Existing Betweeen Frame Factors, Steering Group and Teaching Process Variables

this relation in an example. In order to explain this relation, we shall take a logical link between assumed concepts, with cértain concepts by definition becoming more limited than is actually possible. For the sake of discussion, let us take two different theories or ideals about the directions and contents of education—two General Theories on Education, A and B.

Theory A takes as its starting point that all education has the primary goal of transmitting a culture's 'collective memory' from one generation to the next. By collective memory we mean the systematized knowledge that exists in various sciences. In this way, the general goals become centered upon knowledge, and the sequence of content units is formed according to the structure this knowledge has. It is still possible to imagine variations in the way this knowledge is supplied. This supplying of knowledge must be subordinate to the goals and the sequence, and can be formed only within these frames.

Theory B takes as its starting point that the individual is not only a passive receiver of knowledge. The individual thus determines which system of knowledge is to be supplied. Further, it is not possible to specify, from the very first, what is to be supplied. On the other hand, various teaching methods and sequences between methods can be set up as means to reach the goals. Certain situations are to be arranged, in which the individual is given freedom to choose what is to be learned. In this case, the content becomes what is actually learned, subordinate to the activity in the teaching process.

These two separate starting points give us two separate grounds for determining what we mean by frame factors. For theory A, the goal and the sequence of content, as frame factors, will be determined by the content, and the curriculum (the syllabus) is a detailed expression of this. Within the given frames, we may get a certain variation in activity. For theory B we have an opposite state of affairs, that the frame factors will be determined by the activities suggested by the curriculum.

Lundgren (1987, p 529) brings out the wider implications of his theory as:

> Frame factors are then factors that constrain the teaching process and which are not manipulated by the teachers. In studying the teaching process, it is important to deter-

mine what is possible or not possible within the frames given and how the frames have been built up. The latter demands a historical analysis. Frame factors cannot be seen as simple functions of a rationalistic planning model; they must be understood as residuals of earlier school systems, as consequences of public expenditures, and as expressions of wider economic and political context of education.

References

Lundgren, U.P. (1972): Frame Factors and The Teaching Process, Almqvist & Wiksell, Stockholm.

Lundgren, U.P. (1987): "Frame Factors," *The International Encyclopaedia of Teaching and Teacher Education* ed. Dunkin, M.J. pp. 525-530, Pergamon Press, Oxford.

3.2.20 Stolurow: Socrates—A Computer Based Instructional Model

Stolurow describes a cybernalic computer-based instructional system, SOCRATES (Figure 3.2.21). The acronym, SOCRATES, is System for Organising Content to Review and Teach Educational Subjects. It consists of a group of student input-output (I/O) stations to a digital computer through a relay track. It is a computer-based multiple access, instructional system, designed to meet the requirements of an idiographic contingency model of instructional process.

The model of the teaching-learning process is an idiographic contingency conception. It is based on the assumption that individualised instruction is a multiple-stage decision process which is diagnostic, prescriptive and corrective in its use of psychological information to make decisions about teaching; but the decision process is basically continuous, in which three stages can be identified. In the *first* stage the pre-tutorial decisions are made; in the *second*, the tutorial decisions are made; and in the *third*, the programme revisions are made. In the first two stages there are two levels of operations which make the system highly adaptive to individual differences.

a) Pre-tutorial decision: In the pre-tutorial stage, one set of decisions, determines the assignment of each to an instructional station, the other set determines the educational programme to be used in teaching a student.

The outcome of the pre-tutorial processing is a tutorial programme for each student, based upon data about his aptitudes, abilities and personality.

b) Tutorial Programme: It is made up of two parts: its logic and content. The complete set of rules used in making all of the decisions in teaching a student is the logic of his instruction. The content is the particular set of topics to be taught. It depends on the student's pre-test performance and performance while learning.

Teaching Strategy can be described in terms of two types of rules used in presenting a set of frames. The first type of rules determines sequence on orderly organisations of the frames relating to an objective. The second type of rules specifies the conditions under which the frames are presented, for example, a

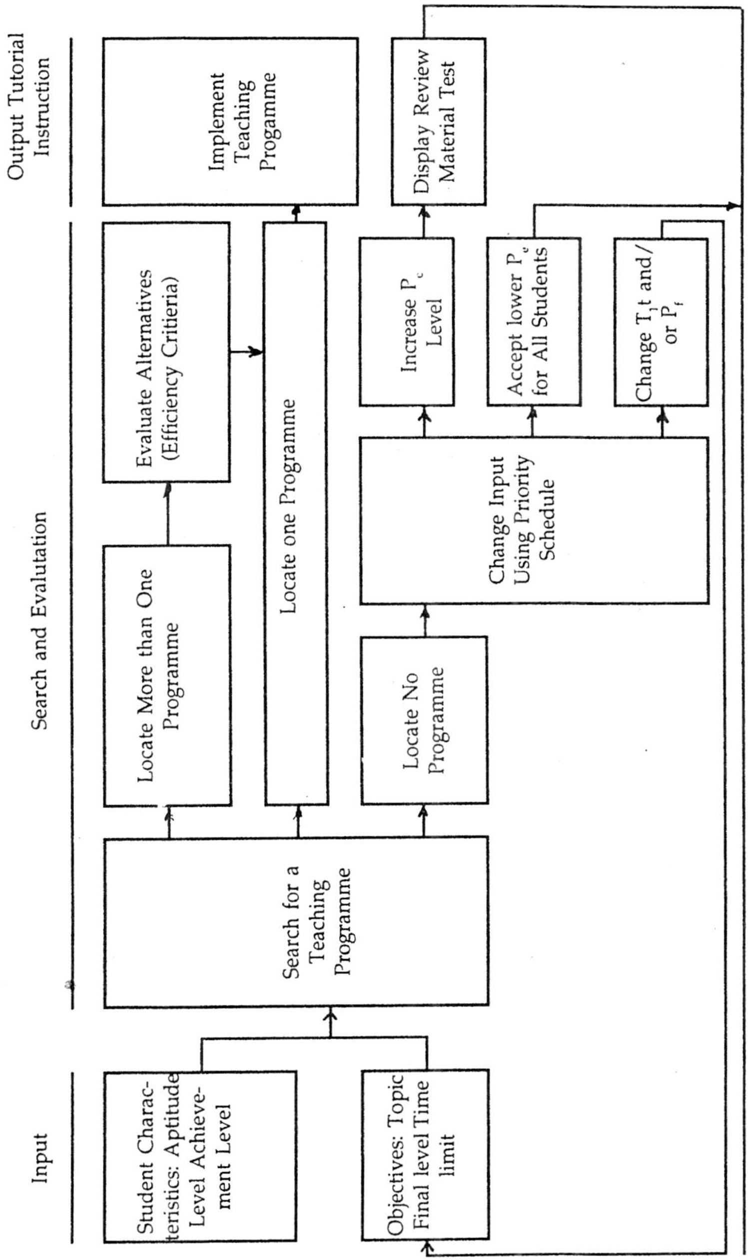

Fig. 3.2.21 A Computer Based Instructional Model (Based on Stolurow)

picture which is a part of a frame may be timed, or the medium used to encode the frame might be a film for some, or an audiotape for others. A complete set of rules includes both types, and the set, employed in teaching a student to reach an objective, is referred to as a 'teaching strategy'. Two levels of tutorial instruction are possible. The lower level is obtained when the system is programmed to teach with a fixed logic and a fixed content, e.g. a linear programme or drill and practice. At this level all the instructional possibilities are 'pre-specified' including the type of feedback given to all students. The higher level is obtained when the system is programmed to alter either its logic or its content, or both, for subsequent parts of the instructional programme on the earlier parts.

c) The third and best way to make the system more adaptive by using a variety of criteria in making decisions is to either maintain or change the instructional rules themselves. There are three ways of programming SOCRATES to determine the level at which the system is being adaptively used. Basically it is programmed to function as a cybernatic system, which uses the response data as input to the system, the response data is used to determine whether or not subsequent change will be made in the operation of the system. The response data are accumulated and the records were related to expected response data values or norms. In this way the system learns about the student as it instructs him.

References

DeCecco, J.P. and Crawford. W. (1977): *The Psychology of Learning and Instruction*, Prentice-Hall of India, New Delhi.

Stolurow, L.M. and Daniel, D. (1965): *Teaching Machines and Computer-Based System, Teaching Machines and Programmed Learning II: Data and Directions*, Ed. R. Glaser, pp. 162-212: Department of Audiovisual Education, National Education Association, Washington, D.C.

CHAPTER FOUR

INDIAN PERSPECTIVE

4.1 MODELS IN RESEARCH AND PRACTICE

A study of Models/Theories of Teaching began in India under the leadership of two outstanding educational scientists in India in 1970s—Shib K. Mitra in the NCERT, New Delhi and M.B. Buch in the CASE, M.S. University, Baroda. Mitra (1970) chose "Psychology of Teaching: Rudiments of a Theory" as his presidential address in Psychology and Educational Science section of 67th Annual Conference of Indian Science Congress at the I.I.T., Kharagpur. He was much influenced by Gage's celebrated 'Handbook'. Buch published his research findings of his actual observation of classrooms in *Communication in Classroom* (1970). He was influenced by Flander's work on 'analysing teaching behaviour' and 'interaction analysis'. Teaching was taken up as a major area of research in the CASE in 1970s and a review of research of theory of teaching was undertaken by S.P. Bhattacharya in 1971 under the guidance of M.B. Buch. In 1972 Buch as Head of CASE organised Third National Seminar on "Research in teaching towards developing a theory of teaching" in January 1972 in which twenty-one educational researchers from 14 universities in India, with experience and expertise in research on teaching, came to participate.

Three national lectures of Shib K. Mitra on 'Psychology of Teaching' were also arranged to synchronize with this national seminar. The Third National Seminar on research in teaching at Baroda reassured the Indian researchers on classroom interaction analysis and teacher behaviour of the soundness of their approach and called upon them to focus their study on the emerging field of Model building in teaching so that in near future models of teaching can be used in Indian classroom conditions and ultimately India can also contribute in building a theory/ theories on teaching. In the subsequent three decades, efforts were made by educational researchers to study classroom behaviours of teachers and how to change their teaching behaviours to increase pupils' cognitive and attitudinal developments. Efforts were also made to identify teaching skills for teaching different subjects and to improve general teaching competence. Different teaching patterns were explored to see their effectiveness and efficacy in increasing pupils' learning. The Publications of Joyce and Well (1980) and Dunkin (1987) tremendously boosted the use of models of teaching in increasing pupils' learning outcomes and relating teaching to the educational as well as the social systems.

Related to Models of Teaching the first study at Ph.D. level was completed in 1983 by U.G. Chitriv—Evaluating Differential Effectiveness of Ausubel and Bruner Strategies for Acquisition of Concepts in Mathematics, Ph.D. Edn., Nag. U., 1983.

By now six Ph.D. studies were completed related to models of teaching. Models like Advance Organiser Model, Inquiry Training Model, Concept Attainment Model, Cognitive Growth Model, the Jurisprudential Inquiry Model and the Nondirective Model have been investigated wherein teaching has been done with the help of models of teaching. Programmed instruction, learning Module and Personalised System of Instruction were the instruction strategies based on operant conditioning model. These teaching techniques were also researched widely in India. Micro-teaching technique is widely researched and practiced in teacher education to develop teaching skills particularly in pre-service teacher trainees.

Passi, Singh and Sansanwal in Indore University in 1985 developed a training strategy to train teacher-educators in models of teaching.

> "The training comprised orientation in the theory of the model, lesson plan guide, teaching analysis guide through lectures and discussion. This was followed by demon-

stration lessons and practice in quadro. The training strategy was found to be effective in terms of theoretical understanding of the model and a favourable change in teacher-educator's reactions towards models of teaching. In this study, the Concept Attainment and Inquiry Training Models were taken up. This strategy was replicated on a different sample of teacher educators in 1986. The models of teaching considered were the Advance Organiser Model and the Jurisprudential Inquiry Models. A national project related the value clarification was completed in March 1988. In this project, the Value Discussion Model and Jurisprudential Inquiry Model were studied. This project was completed by the Department of Education, Devi Ahilya Vishwavidyalaya, Indore, in collaboration with the Department of Teacher Education, Special Education and Extension Services, NCERT, New Delhi. Again in 1988, a new batch of teacher educators were trained in the Value Analysis Model for studying its impact on the value clarification ability of student-teachers. New models of teaching are being investigated, new indigenous training approaches have been designed. The only Ph.D. study related to training has been by Awasthi (1988) who found that the Continuous Demonstration with Pair Practice (CDP) strategy and Intermittent Demonstration with the Quadro Practice (IDP) strategy were found to be equally effective in terms of theoretical understanding of the Concept Attainment Model, while in terms of teaching competence, the IDP-Practice strategy was significantly superior to the CDP-Practice strategy."

(*Passi & Sansanwal*, 1991)

Reference

Passi, B.K. and Sansanwal, D.N. (1991): "Research in Teaching—A Trend Report" in Buch, M.B. (Ed.) *Fourth Survey of Research in Education*, Vol. II, NCERT, New Delhi.

CHAPTER FIVE

CONCLUSION

Issues in Building Models of Teaching

The importance of a model of teaching was clearly brought out by Gage (1972) relating the concept of teaching with its related activities as given below:

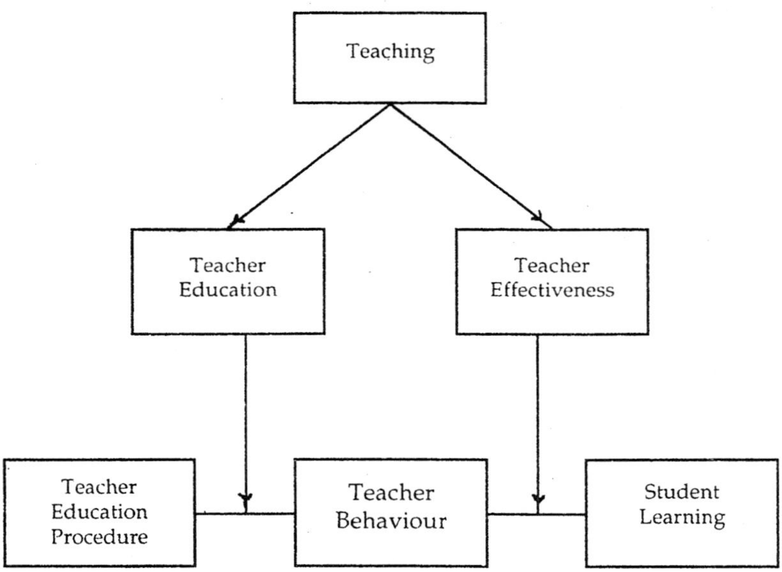

Fig. 5.1 Teaching and its Related Activities

The model of teaching implies concepts, principles, procedures and products of all these activities.

Recent researches on building models of teaching have highlighted some aspects of the components of Figure 5.1. Some major *issues* are given below:

5.1 TEACHING: ART OR SCIENCE ?

There exists a debate whether teaching is an art or a science. The debate has its origin in issues as to whether teaching can be researched empirically and whether teachers can be trained scientifically.

According to Highet (1954) teaching is not a science, it is an art, principally because it involves human beings, their emotions and values which he regarded as "quite outside the grasp of science". He argued:

> "It seems to me very dangerous to apply the aims and methods of science to human beings as individ-uals.... Teaching involves emotions, which cannot be systematically appraised and employed, and human values, which are quite outside the grasp of Science.... "Scientific teaching, even of scientific subjects, will be inadequate as long as both teachers and pupils are human beings."

To Gage (1964) the important issue is whether scientific methods can be used in understanding more about teaching. Whether teaching is an art or a science is a most controversial question. He argued that all human activities, including artistic ones, have "inherent order and lawfulness" that make them quite suitable for scientific analysis. Further Gage (1978) commented that teaching is a vast continuum in its nature; it is at best *'practical art'*.

The real issue that confronts the researchers and teachers is to understand teaching through the application of scientific methods. The problem is of building a scientific, objective edifice of teaching that goes on in classroom instruction, group discussion, tutorials and distance learning.

5.2 LOGICAL STRUCTURE

The concept of 'cognitive structure' as formulated by Bruner (1966) and Ausubel (1967), 'learning structure' of Gagne (1965) and 'logic tree' of Hickey and Newton (1964), whatever their variations in vocabulary and detail, are similar ideas and they ought to be assimilated into one another in building a model of teaching.

5.3 SEQUENCING

Again, the concepts of the instructional process as 'cyclical give-and-take' by Smith (1963), Runkle-Stone-Leavitt as cited by Gage (1963), a pattern of 'structuring-soliciting-responding-reacting' as described by Bellack and his associates (1966) and 'a sequence of stimulus-response-reinforcement' as formulated by the programmed instruction school of Skinner (1953), Stolurow (1965) and others have common elements in them. These sequences ought to be recognised as such as brought together into the model.

5.4 FEEDBACK

The works of Skinner, teaching machine and the subsequent developments in computer and modes of teaching have emphasised the role of feedback in a model of instruction.

> "Feedback" essentially means a "...a part of the communication output fed back again into the input channel to monitor or modulate the communication process itself, such as to improve accuracy of message transmission, reduce level of noise, increase channel capacity and so on." In learning theory, 'knowledge or result' has been used as a form of reinforcement.

5.5 PRE-TUTORIAL PHASE: LEARNING OBJECTIVES

The study of models of teaching has highlighted in pedagogy. It is the first component of Glaser's 'Basic Teaching Model'. The importance of instructional objectives in teaching-learning situation was first pointed out by Tyler, a curriculum theorist, in 1949 following the famous 'Tyler Rationale'.

a) What educational purposes should the school seek to attain?
b) What educational experiences can be provided that are likely to attain these purposes?
c) How can these educational experiences be effectively organised?
d) How can we determine whether these purposes are being achieved?

Thereafter Mager (1962) developed the technique of programmed instruction demanding that learning objectives should be specified in *behavioural terms*. In recent times Popham (1969) brought a balance between the Tylerian generality and Mager's specificity. Hilda Taba (1962) also used objectives in curriculum construction in the pre-tutorial phase of instruction.

5.6. TEACHER'S EXPECTATION

Rosenthal and Jackobson opened up a new paradigm in teaching where they related teacher's expectations with pupils' academic achievement.

Teacher's expectancies is another potential explanation of the poorer academic achievement of high communication apprehensive students. Since the publication of *Pygmalion in the Classroom* (Rosenthal & Jackobson 1968), there has been increased interest in the effects of teachers' expectations on the achievement of their students.

5.7. META-ANALYTIC STUDIES IN MODELS OF TEACHING

A family of Models is concerned with classroom interaction (Bellack, 1966; Flanders, 1965; Dunkin & Biddle, 1974 and Gage, 1978). Out of these studies the basic instructional behaviours are identified as "Teacher structuring", "Soliciting", "Responding" and "Reacting".

These patterns are amusingly similar all-over the developed countries (Dahllof and Lundgren 1970). On the other hand making a kind of meta-analysis of all existing studies on "Teacher behaviour and student achievement paradigm" Gage broadly identified four basic teaching acts, namely:

a) Cognitive Organization
b) Indirectness
c) Warmth
d) Enthusiasm

Since teachers must continue to operate in advance of a data base, they must become aware of researchers who identify the basic skills of teaching which they may try and test in their classrooms. The role of the teacher, then, becomes that of an action researcher and problem-solver. In exercising this role, teachers need to be aware of the most recent theory and research on instruction as a means of enlarging the number and quality of options available for teaching. It is important that teachers are aware that nine variables have yielded consistent results across the fifty-odd studies in which naturally occurring teacher behaviours were related to measures of student growth (Rosenshine & Furst, 1973). These are:

i) Clarity
ii) Variability
iii) Enthusiasm
iv) Task oriented and/or business-like attitude
v) Criticism
vi) Teacher indirectness
vii) Student opportunity to learn criterion materials
viii) Use of structuring comments, and
ix) Multiple levels of questions or cognitive discourse.

Rosenshine and Furst's nine variables, then, are nine dimensions of classroom communication which teachers can try and test in their classroom.

5.8. MODEL(S) OF TEACHING: GLOBAL OR MULTIPLE

Another basic problem in developing a theory of teaching is concerned with whether there should be global theory of teaching or multiple theories of teaching. In this view multiple theories of teaching will result from the effects of the researchers and each theory of teaching will offer explanation of limited aspects of teaching variations depending upon the nature of subject matter and kind of students taught. Hermanoweiez (1965) saw the importance of multi-theories of teaching as constituting:

> "a corpus of knowledge with demonstrable power to describe, explain and control various dimensions of teaching...such knowledge also will provide greater classification on the points of convergence and relevance of ancillary disciplines like psychology, sociology and philosophy to the educational process."

Bruner (1966) by implication and Travers (1966) in his outspoken manner had advocated for a theory of instruction which is comprehensive, scientific and all inclusive. Smith too, in recent years, has spoken of a meta-theory of teaching.

Teachers teach students of differentiated aptitude, ability and social class—a large number of subjects at several levels. The need is, therefore, several models of teaching at substantive level. But the ultimate goal should be an all-embracing 'Theory of Teaching' at meta-level.

5.9 TOWARDS A NEW PHILOSOPHY OF A MODEL OF TEACHING

Most of the 'Models of Teaching' are learner-centred. But this learner centredness was given a new meaning by Lewin in his formulation B = f(PxE), i.e. Behaviour (B) is a function (f) of interaction (X) between person (P) and environment (E). Paulo Freire in his *Pedagogy of the Oppressed* (1972) gave a Philosophical model of teaching where the learner discovers his curriculum by meaningful dialogue with the teacher accompanied by thoughtful analysis and interpretation of the findings. Teaching is an *action verb* to grow awareness and end in realisation. In Freire's terms Teaching means realisation of the social, poilitical and economic contradictions in the world where the learner lives, and the initiating action individually or in groups to improve by changing the existing condition. It is, therefore, a process of developing knowledge, beliefs and motives so that a person can attend autonomy and self-responsibility. It is 'conscientization'. According to Illich; I.D. *Tools for conviviality* (1973), teaching should be a spontaneous, self-selected and self-directed activity. He accuses present teaching as a narrow professionalism of teachers that safeguards their qualifications, professional certification and status. The three corner-stones of teaching will be survival, justice and self-defined work. Conviviality in teaching would entail the recognition of the uniqueness and worth of each person, when he learns through his own activities in natural environments and events. He charges present teaching as being like the guarded skills of the medieval closed guild system.

Finally, the most exciting field in the ideology of a theory of teaching is opened up by Habermas, *Legitimation Crisis* (1976) through his theory of *communicative action* which considers teaching as a critical function. In interaction between the teacher and the taught there are two actions, 'Strategic action' and 'Communicative action'. In communicative action, the teacher and the students search for a common truth, a validity judgement for mutual understanding. According to him an utterance of a teacher has three meanings, namely to represent something in the word, to express the speaker's intention and to establish legitimacy (Validity judgement for objective criteria). So far in all pedagogic transactions, we have considered the first two by cognitive analysis and ideological stands. But legitimacy at the level of judgement had not been attempted in human interaction. A model of teaching should, therefore, search for legitimizing the acts of teaching.

References

Ausubel, D.P. (1986): *Educational Psychology: A Cognitive View*, Holt, Pinchart & Winston, New York.

Bellack, A.A. et. al. (1966): *The Language of the Classroom*, Teachers College Press, New York.

Bruner, J.S. (1966): *Toward a Theory of Instruction*, Harvard University Press, Cambridge, Mass.

Dahllof, U. & Lundgren, U.P. (1970): *Macro and Micro Approaches Combined for Curriculum Process Analysis: A Swedish Field Project*, Paper read at the AERA meeting in Minneapolis 2-6 March; Reports from the Institute of Education No. 10, University of Goteborg, Goteborg (Mimeo).

Dunkin, M.J. & Biddle, B.J. (1974): *The Study of Teaching*, Holt, Rinehart & Winston, New York.

Flanders, N.A. (1965): *Teacher Influence, Pupil Attitude, and Achievement: Studies in Interaction Analysis*, U.S. Office of Education, Co-operative Research Project No 397, University of Minnesota, Minneapolis.

Gage, N.L. (1963): *Handbook of Research on Teaching*. Rand McNally, Chicago.

Gage, N.L. (1964): "Theories of Teaching," in *Theories of Learning and Instruction*, Chap. XI, 63rd. Year book of National Society for the Study of Education, Part II, Washington, D.C.

Gage, N.L. (1972): *Teacher Effectiveness and Teacher Education*, Pacific Books Publishers, California.

Gage, N.L. (1978): *The Scientific Basis of the Art of Teaching*, Teachers College Press, New York.

Gagne, R.M. (1965): *The Conditions of Learning*, Holt, Rinehart and Winston, New York.

Hermanoweiez, W.J. (1965): "Studies of Teaching and Their Impact on Future Developments of Teacher Education." Conference paper, Indiana.

Hickey, A. and Newton, J.M. (1964): The Logical Basis of Teaching: The effect of sub-concept sequence in learning, *Final Report of Office of Naval Research*, Personnel and Training Branch, Contract No. 4215.

Highet, G. (1954): *The Art of Teaching*, Vintage Books, New York.

Mager, R.F. (1962): *Preparing Objectives for Programmed Instruction*, Fearon Pub., Pals Alto, Calif.

Popham, W.J. (1969): 'Objectives and Instruction' in Popham, W.J. et. al. (Eds.) *Instructional Objectives*, AERA Monograph, Rand McNally, Washington, D.C.

Rosenshine, B. & Furst, N. (1973): The Use of Direct observation to study Teaching, in Travers, R.M.W.(Ed.) *Second Handbook of Research on Teaching*, A Project of AERA, Rand McNally, Chicago.

Skinner, B.F. (1953): *Science and Human Behaviour*, Macmillan, Inc., New York.

Smith, B.O. (1963): "Towards A Theory of Teaching," in Bellack, A.A.(Ed.), *Theory and Research in Teaching*, Bureau of Publications, Teachers College, Columbia University, New York.

Taba, H. (1962): *Curriculum Development*, Harcourt, Brace and World, New York.

Travers, R.W. (1966): "Towards Taking the Fun out of Building a Theory of Instruction," *Teachers College Record*.

BASIC READINGS

1. Allen D.W. & Ryan K.A., *Micro-teaching*, Reading, Mass Addison Wesley, 1969.
2. Anderson R.C. & others, *Current Research on Instruction* Englewood Cliffs. N.J. Prentice-Hall, 1969.
3. Barker L.L., *Communication in the Classroom*, Englewood Cliffs, N.J. Prentice-Hall, 1982.
4. Bhattacharya S.P., *Review of Research on Theory of Teaching* Baroda, CASE, M.S. Univ., 1973.
5. Biddle B.J. & Ellena W.J. (Eds.), *Contemporary Research on Teacher Effectiveness*, New York, Rinehart and Winston, 1964.
6. Block J.H. & Anderson L.W., *Mastery Learning in Classroom Instruction*, New york, Macmillan, 1975.
7. Bloom B.S., *Human Characteristics and School Learning*, New York, McGraw-Hill, 1976.
8. Bropny J., *Recent Research on Teaching*, East Lansing, Institute for Research on Teaching, Michigan State University, 1980.
9. Joyce B. & Weil M., Models of Teaching, New Delhi, Prentice-Hall of India Pvt. Ltd. 1992 (4th Ed.).
10. Bruner J.S., *Toward a Theory of Instruction*, Cambridge, Harvard University Press, 1969.
11. Buch M.B. & Santhanam M.R., *Communication in Classroom*, Baroda CASE, M.S. Univ. 1970.
12. Dunkin M.J. (Ed.), *The International Encyclopaedia of Teaching and Teacher Education*, Oxford Pergamon Press, 1987.
13. Dunkin M.J. & Biddle B.J., *The Study of Teaching*, New York Halt, Rinehart and Winston, 1974.

14. Gage N.L., Theories of teaching. In: Hilgard E.R. (Ed.) *Theories of Learning and Instruction*, National Society for the Study of Education year Book No. 63, Part-I. Chicago, Illinois, Chicago Press, 1964.
15. Gage N.L., *The Scientific Basis of the Art of Teaching*, New York, Teachers College Press, 1978.
16. Gage N.L., *Teacher Effectiveness and Teacher Education*, Palo Allo, Calif Pacific Books, 1972.
17. Gage N.L. (Ed.), *Handbook of Research on Teaching*, Chicago, Rand McNally, 1963.
18. Hadden E.E., *Evolving Instruction*, New York, Macmillan, 1970.
19. Hyman R.T., Contemporary Thoughts on Teaching Englewood Cliffs, N.J. Prentice Hall, 1971.
20. Lundgren U.P., *Frame Factors and the Teaching Process;* A Contribution to Curriculum Theory and Theory on Teaching. Stockholm, Almqirst and Wiksell, 1972.
21. MacDonald J.B. & Leeper R.E. (Ed.), *Theories on Instruction* Washington D.C. National Education Associations, 1965.
22. Nuthall G. & Snook I., Contemporary Models of Teaching. In: Travers R.M.W. (Ed.) *Second Handbook of Research on Teaching* Chicago, Rand McNally, 1973.
23. Passi B.K. & Sansarwal D.N., Research in Teaching—A Trend Report in Buch M.B. (Ed.) *Fourth Survey of Research in Education* (1983-88), New Delhi, N.C.E.R.T. 1991.
24. Siddique M.H. & Khan M.S., *Models of Teaching*—Theory and Research, New Delhi, Ashish Publishing House, 1991.
25. Siegal L. (Ed.), *Instruction: Some Contemporary View Points.* Sanfrancisco, Chandler, 1967.
26. Skinner B.F., *The Technology of Teaching*, New York, Appleton Century Crafts, 1969.
27. Smith B.O. (Ed.), *Research in Teacher Education*, Symposium AERA, Englewood Cliff, N.J. Prentice-Hall Inc., 1971.
28. Walberg H.J. & Peterson P.L. (Ed.), *Research on Teaching*: Concepts, Findings and Implications, Barkeley, Colif, McCutchar, 1979.